HOW TO GROW A BEARD
A MILITARY TRANSITION GUIDE BACK INTO CIVILIAN LIFE

R. GRAVES

This book is dedicated to all my brothers and sisters in the Armed Forces. You are truly heroes whether you worked in the chow hall, or fought on the front lines. The love and respect I have for what you do and have done (on the grander scale of things) is immeasurable.

This book is also dedicated to the friends and family I have lost because of the war, depression, and suicide. You will forever live through the stories we tell of you, and the memories you gave to us. Rest in Peace.

Acknowledgements

　　　　I would like to thank my friends and military family, for being a large part of who I am today. It took me many years to find my family, but from the day I met each and every one of you, I was blessed to be a part of you, as you have been a part of me.

Fraijos- So, so many years of ups and downs. So many years of uncertainty, and success. So much history between me and both adults in your home, and I wouldn't have it any other way! I wouldn't be able to write this book if it weren't for your belief in me and your ability to put your name and neck out on the line for me. Truly my best friends, and I hope our lives extend into the afterworld that you so direly do not believe in Chris.

Cordero- Wipe that shit off your head! I would listen to your ridiculous rules over and over again about how I need to basically get out of the house and leave you alone if the yellow towel is hanging on the couch, if listening to those stupid rules allows me to have you in my life as close as we've become. Thank you for believing in me, and boosting my confidence while at all time lows.

Big Chris- **YOU** broke the shackles! Thank you!

Arleen- I want to thank you—my wife—for really believing in me when I didn't believe in myself. Thank you for really holding down our lives at home when I was away for so long. You never were a military spouse but you basically lived the life. I told you December 31st 2014, as you were rocking our son to sleep as the clock struck midnight, that we would remember that moment as a new beginning, and here we are today. You are my strength and my weakness, my lover, and my companion. You are my wife and my best friend, and because of you—I can.

More than anything, I would like to *sincerely* thank Michael "Mad Dog Mike" Washington. A 30(ish)-year-old me looks back on my time in the Marine Corps, and ultimately I am grateful to have had you in my life. You are the epitome of what a Marine, a man, a father, a husband, a friend, and a brother should be. I learned to be who I am today because of you, and I can never express exactly how grateful I am for you to have put your neck out there for me so many times, and for leading by example. You taught me humility, patience, professionalism, and the power of a second (third, fourth, and possibly fifth) chance. You never asked to be anyone's hero, but I promise you—you are many of ours. Thank you Wash. "JEYEAH"

Finally I'd like to dedicate this book to my son Jacob. Let your imagination run free, and do great things in this world. Never let your dreams be forgotten or ridiculed. You are meant to do something very special in this world, and I love you with an undying love. I hope I never fail you as a father and I pray I set the best example a father could set for his son. May you live a long and meaningful life, and know that you are loved beyond the limits of love.

To all the other amazing people I've come across in my life, Max, Mark, Harrells, TJ & Lyric, Top Stevens, everyone in Radar, OPS, and TDS (MACS Units Stand Tall), my ITT gang, my dive family, and my college familia... every moment I had with you, I cherish.

A big thank you to the HMI squad, you have helped me get to a place in my life where I can truly blossom and give back to something greater than myself.

Believe me, if you are not mentioned you are thought of often. I'd have to write a whole book of thank you's for all the people who have made an impact in my life. I'll never forget the Marines I served with, and the people I came across while serving. You were a huge part of my life, and as it stood while we served together, I will still always be in your corner through the good and bad.

Last but not least, I want to thank God for continuing to place me in positions of learning, and leadership. I owe so much to you for watching over me for so long.

How to Grow a Beard

Table of Contents

Acknowledgements	3
GOOD MORNING MARINES I AM ROBERT GRAVES AND I WILL BE GIVING YOU THIS PERIOD OF INSTRUCTION!	9
How To Use This Book	15
Discovering the Path	17
Your Military Rate, AFSC, or MOS	25
Don't Burn Bridges	31
Acronyms	39
Join a Small Group	45
Know Your Worth	53
How to Find a Job That's Right for You	61
Wrapping up Loose Ends	75
Who Are You? Who Am I?	83
It's Time for Lunch	89
"I've Never Been Treated Like This in my Life"	93
Find Yourself a Mentor	101
A Lesson in Humility	105
Leave Your Potty Mouths in the Shitter	111
Call the Pro's	115
Sacrifice	129
Do Something for You	135
Get Fixed!	141
It's Ok to Swallow Your Pride	149
Life After a Court-Martial	155
How to Grow a Beard	165
Appendix	170

How to Grow a Beard

INTRODUCTION

GOOD MORNING MARINES I AM ROBERT GRAVES AND I WILL BE GIVING YOU THIS PERIOD OF INSTRUCTION!

If you had asked me in November of 1999, I would've told you to get out of my face with the thought of enlisting in any branch of service. In fact I think I told my mother verbatim, "fuck that... I'm not joining the military." However, just days later on December 31st 1999, I signed the proverbial dotted line that many of us remember so vividly. At the time, one of my best friends was home on boot leave and my other *bff* who had already been talking about enlisting, had already enlisted and was leaving for boot camp right after we'd graduate from high school. I had torn my ligaments in my ankle earlier that year, taking me out of competition for any chance I had at a sports scholarship, and so in true Graves' fashion, without second thought—I walked into the recruiting station around the corner from the movie theatre, I watched the recruiting videos, went and took the ASVAB at MEPS, picked an MOS, and had the recruiter asking my mom for her signature (because I was seventeen) all in the span of a day.

The Marine Corps was the best thing that ever happened to me. Where my mother still to this day swears I've been brainwashed, the truth is, I've never known what a true family was until I joined the Corps. In the Corps I met life long friends, I had coaches and leaders who were readily available to figuratively and literally put their foot in my ass and keep me in line. I picked up bad habits, broke other bad habits, put on some muscle, gained a beer belly, got in fights, traveled the world, got into a shit load of trouble, helped people with their individual and family problems, created life long stories, served my country and the servicemen and women beside me, but most importantly… I grew up. I became a man. I eventually—through all that, became a responsible adult.

True of me in the Marine Corps, as I was before it, I was never the quiet one—waiting on the sideline for something to happen. I always volunteered for things (other than working parties) and in essence I learned new skills, and was privileged to encounter a variety of experiences outside of working in my shop. Because of my assertiveness, I learned a lot of useful tools and functions that helped me interact fluidly with other servicemen and women, senior leadership, civilian contractors, educators, local nationals—really, anyone that I came in contact with.

I took pride in myself—knowing that I could walk into most anyone's office, and not be treated like a subordinate or a lower-grade Marine. Because of this "freedom," I was able to help my Marines out when they needed anything, with very little resistance from my command. The more I interacted with the professionals, the more professional I felt, and the more lead-way I had around my unit to help others. And I did. I would go out of my way to do anything for my fellow Marine, and I never held onto any type of knowledge for personal gain. And that's most likely where this book comes from.

As a Staff Sergeant select I was involved in a fight in Okinawa Japan that changed the path of my life forever. Even though I was offered NJP two separate times, I opted to stand up for my innocence in a Court Martial. Stupid you say right? Well, no. As the ones who make the military their career are well aware of, there are limited slots for re-enlistment and all that fun stuff, and unfortunately I was in an MOS that *any* blemish on your record would keep you from re-enlisting if you hadn't made E-6 yet, and if you had made E-6, you'd NEVER EVER BE PROMOTED AGAIN… no matter how stellar you were. Just ask my friends Mark and Sue-Lynn.

I knew what my involvement in the fight was, and my ultimate dream was to become a Marine Corps Warrant Officer, and the only way that could happen was to keep my name clean. And so I fought. And I lost that fight. I was busted down from Sergeant to Lance Corporal but fortunately I never served any jail time in the brig, maintained my clearance, was able to finish my contract, and was discharged honorably. I even got my blood stripes back after I'd picked up Corporal some months later. Not once during that whole time did anyone ever speak down to me or treat me like a piece of shit—I was still seen as Sgt. Graves to the community. It spoke volumes of who I was and what affect I had on the people I had come across.

That meant the world to me.

I now am a civilian. Once I got out of the Marine Corps I got a job in the same field of work I was working in while serving, and having grown tired of fixing radars and traveling on the road away from my family months at a time, I decided to pursue my curiosity of the human brain; specifically behavior modification. I finished my Bachelor Degree in Psychology, and then studied hypnotherapy for a year and became a Certified Hypnotherapist in hopes that I can help people more effectively on their paths to become who they want to be, but are having a hard time figuring out how to achieve their goals—or in veterans' cases—having a hard time fitting in.

I have a great job, a wife whom I love to death and a baby boy (in opposition to the radar MOS myth of not being able to have boys since we worked around radiation). But my reason for writing this book isn't to gloat, or sit up on a high horse of who I've become... no. My purpose of writing this book is to help my brothers, sisters, and your families to have a successful transition back into a world that will never fully understand us, and frankly, isn't ready for you.

As servicemen and women, *we are* a different breed of human. We have specialized training in specific areas, but we're also team players, motivators, self-initiators, and leaders. The best part is whether or not you were cream of the crop, or just someone waiting out their time for the ability to use their college benefits, you will inevitably see an enormous difference between you and the average civilian. We know how to think outside of the box, and we know what accomplishing the mission is all about. However our mission is different in the civilian world… our mission out here is to survive and succeed among people who will never understand us.

HOW TO GROW A BEARD

How To Use This Book

Whether you're just getting in the service, just coming out, or have been out for a while now... this book has something for everyone. I'll share everything I've learned to become successful in the civilian world, as well as being successful in a different type of career, having a family life, and returning home to your friends. Remember—nothing is the same as you remember. The transition from the military may feel like the transition from hero to zero, or you may leave and feel like the rest of the world owes you something. Whatever your mentality is like when you receive your DD-214, my goal is to help you make your transition as successful as possible.

Each chapter will focus on some stage of the beginning years of my military career, followed by being reoriented as a civilian. I will talk about key points of what to do before getting out, what to do right after you get out, and how to get on track with getting a decent paying job, a house, and help you set yourself up right from the start instead of having you have to learn from mistakes that many of the veterans before you have made. Haven't we done enough of that?

As you read through the chapters, make notes in the blank spaces of what you need to do for yourself, highlight key points, and dog ear the pages at will!

Remember, knowledge is power. Use this book as a <u>guide</u> for success in becoming a civilian. There are no more periods of military instruction after you get out. There will be no more Staff Sergeants or Chiefs to protect you from the big green weenie once you're out. No, once you're out there's a whole new beast to conquer—life outside the cammies.

DISCOVERING THE PATH

I was born in Birmingham, Alabama and raised everywhere else. That's what I tell people when they ask me where I'm from, because it's true. From Birmingham we moved to Houston, Dallas, Las Vegas, all over Southern California, and the last place I remember myself with both parents before they split—a house in North Hollywood. You see, my dad was "old south"... you know—a *women-and-kids-are-to-be-seen-not-heard* type of guy, and he had no problem reminding both my mother and I of his mantra.

At some point when I was four years old, my mother had enough of his shit and woke me up in the middle of the night, had me grab whatever I could hold in my hands (which as a small child who had just been awoken in the middle of the night was a teddy bear and my blanket), and we left that house. That would be the start of our new life.

My mother, being a single mother now, had to play the role of father and mother, which I'm sure was not easy for her to do. She also did the thing that single parents tend to do, which is to try to be their child's best friend. So between the disciplinary hat she wore, and the "cool mom" hat that she wore, my standards growing up were loose, until they weren't. What I mean by that is that one minute I'm outside playing with my friends all day—all weekend, not really having to answer to anyone, and the next minute I'm scrubbing the kitchen floor with a toothbrush. One day I'm the best kid on the block, the next I'm on my knees with my nose in a corner for what was probably fifteen minutes, even though those fifteen minutes seemed like an eternity. I was seemingly always grounded, writing "standards" (remember those?), being yelled at, blamed for something I did or didn't do, whooped, or just being disciplined for *something*. Half the time guilty, and the other half, being forced to suffer through it.

As I grew up, I was sent to live with my dad during the summer, or even in the middle of a school year if my mom felt I was just completely out of control. Moving back and forth took me to Atlanta, Orlando, Maryland, Queens, New York, and back through Los Angeles county once again… hence the *"growing up every where else."* But I settled down in Culver City, which is now where I call home. It was here that I stayed in one school district long enough to make lifelong friends whom I now call family. It was here that I started making my own money at the age of twelve. It was here that I started having long-term girlfriends, and I was interested in playing school and club sports.

It was also here that I learned to how to drink, smoke cigarettes, marijuana, and meth.

As a parent now, I know that the day my mother found out her son was addicted to speed—that it was the scariest thing she'd ever come across. However she held her cool, and forced me to go to Narcotics Anonymous, and seek out help. But she still gave me room to grow and learn, and soon I had a stable foundation of trust again in the home. So as you can imagine, she had to play good cop *and* bad cop, but whatever went down, she made sure I had a strong work ethic, had a strong sense of resilience, and that I was ready to go out into the world.

Our relationship took a huge turn one day after a huge fight over money. You see, my father had died when I was seventeen, and at the time I was working full time at Quiznos, playing sports in high school, maintaining over a 3.0 G.P.A, and I had a steady, serious girlfriend. I even had side jobs with an event planner that I was making $20/hr from, working sometimes until 3:00 a.m on school nights. Not understanding the rules of the Social Security office, she made me cut my hours down at work in order to receive my father's benefits to help with the bills around the house. I abided.

However it turns out everything she told me was unnecessary, and it effected me because as a working teen I was providing a lot of my own lifestyle from the money I earned. I mean… I had to make sure my girlfriend was spoiled, keep gas in the car, and keep my beeper on… the important stuff.

Quizno's had recently gone under new management around the same time my father's funeral was scheduled, and I had asked to have my hours cut because of what my mother understood to be true, and also so I could attend my father's funeral in Birmingham, Alabama. Soon after I returned and found out that my mother was *not* correct about my specific situation with the Social Security offices, I walked into Quiznos and asked my new manager to have my hours reinstated, explaining the unnecessary reasoning for having my hours cut. The new manager could care less and would give me an hour a week for the next month, essentially forcing me out of the job. Taking that tremendous pay cut had certainly affected my way of living. I was unable to keep up on the small bills I had been responsibly taking care of, and my pockets were getting lighter—fast.

Needless to say, I'd brought up the money issue to my mother. I'd questioned the Social Security money situation, and like the unpredictable earthquakes that we are so accustomed to in California, out of nowhere my mother strikes—and this was the big one I'd been waiting for. Asking my mother where my father's Social Security money was, caused my mother to lose it and essentially got me kicked out of my home, and forced to figure life out immediately—so close to graduation.

And I did figure it out. I slept at friend's homes; I shared a bachelor apartment with two other guys that I had met from my girlfriend's church. I even picked up more work from other places in order to maintain my lifestyle, and things were fine.

Soon after the fight, I had a conversation on the phone with my mother. She was giving me the normal verbal lashing, and she'd mentioned, "you should just join the fucking military, it might make you grow the fuck up," to which I replied, "fuck that, I'll never join the military…"

No clear reason why I said that. I had no special hatred against the military or even a reason to react the way I had. But those are the words that immediately flowed out of me at the time, most likely an immediate defiant response mode because at that time in my life, she was the enemy.

You see, my best friend had enlisted, went through boot camp, and was back home on boot leave for the Christmas holidays. My other best friend had signed the papers already, and he was waiting for the school year to finish so he could be on his way to stand on those yellow footprints. Me? I had always thought I was going to play college sports. However, that dream didn't become a reality just because I really didn't have anyone knowledgeable on my side about the recruitment process for college sports scholarships. Not to mention I'd torn my ankle ligaments my senior season. So I started actually thinking about the possibility of enlisting, and since both of my best friends had enlisted in the

Marine Corps, it was only logical that I solidify our bond by doing the same.

I'd talked to my girlfriend at the time to see if she thought it was a good idea for me to enlist. You know... that conversation where you think you're going to stay together forever. The one where you promise the world to your significant other, and that you proclaim, "I'm doing this for us..." *THAT* convo! Well it didn't take much for her to say yes, and no more than mere days after having that telephone conversation with my mother declaring "fuck the military," I walked into the United States Marine Corps recruiting office, talked to Sgt. Ruiz, and told him, "Ok, I want to blow shit up!"

That was December 31st, 1999.

September 11th, 2000 my friend and I stepped on those yellow footprints and changed our lives forever. That day we immediately became different people.

Even though boot camp is just a memory in my far off past now, that is an experience nobody ever forgets. The best part about it was (and by best part I mean worst part), I was *the* tallest recruit in all MCRD. So believe that when I stood out, I stood *out*. What made boot camp worse for me is that I have this nervous reaction that when I'm nervous or uncertain—I smile or laugh, so it was very hard for me to learn how to keep a straight face. You'd think enough trips to the quarterdeck would of broke me of that, but it definitely didn't.

There was a moment in boot camp that paved the way for my thought processes for the future I'd come into in the military. During one brutal quarterdeck visit that pushed me to the breaking point of tears, Sgt. Lorret—a man of leprechaun stature stood right in my face and said in his raspy Drill Instructor voice, "I bet you hate me Graves, don't you, you fucking hate me don't you?!?" To which this recruit replied, "THIS RECRUIT DOES NOT HATE THE DRILL INSTRUCTOR SIR! THIS RECRUIT KNOWS THAT THE DRILL INSTRUCTOR IS JUST DOING HIS JOB SIR!"

You see, other than the physical demand of boot camp, the rest was cake for me. There was *no* amount of being asked to speak up, cleaning, ironing, or doing things in a unnecessary repetitive action that I wasn't ready for—simply because of growing up in the home of my mother. When we were told to do things, I did them. When we were expected not to do things, I didn't. I will stand by this until my dying day: *My mother prepared me for boot camp*! And for those of you who have been through Marine Corps boot camp, that should paint the picture real well of how I was raised.

And so, the story of my military learning's had begun.

Remember: *Everyone has their own "starting-point" story. Life is a journey, and that journey never stops and is never predictable. Embrace all change, and learn to pull something positive from whatever it is you find yourself going through. That's the key to being successful.*

Your Military Rate, AFSC, or MOS

Even though I told my recruiter I wanted to "blow shit up," I apparently scored too high on my ASFAB and got stuck in a job fixing air surveillance radar systems. I was stuck with the nerds of the Marine Corps, which looking back now—was more beneficial in the long run, but I still wish I'd gotten to blow some stuff up.

That fifteen minutes in the recruiters office talking about our future jobs in the service comes and goes so quickly that unfortunately none of us *really truly* knew what we were getting into. I know for a fact that everyone in my MOS thought we were going to fix airplanes and go to MOS school in Pensacola, Florida—only to end up in the much more extravagant Twenty-Nine Palms, California. I mean... I'll take Lake Bandini and running up sand dunes over sunny beaches and bathing suits any day of the week.

Either way, what that tells me is that the recruiters didn't even know what they were peddling to us. All they knew is they had quotas to fill, and if you were an Alpha (on the ASFAB) you were getting a job for someone in your score range; and if you were not an Alpha, the service life could be a little rougher for you. All I knew is that my wish to blow things to little pieces wasn't going to be my reality.

As I mentioned earlier, my MOS school was in Twenty-Nine Palms, and the Marines in my class and occupations similar to mine were stationed there for just shy over a year. The blueprint of the Marine Corps Communication-Electronics School was to teach all the Marines basic electronics, and soldering. Then to separate you from those general classes to our specific occupational schools, in which I learned basic RADAR fundamentals, and then more specific system theory and component level troubleshooting. Being that I was a kid who took things like the toaster and TV apart to see how they worked, I realized that this was going to be a pretty cool job for me.

As the years went on, some of us showed more interest than others, and those that did, excelled at our job. The fortunate got to request to get sent to various trainings on new gear or upgrades, and the "lucky nerds" got stationed at MCTSSA (which was the playground of all the cool new tech stuff being tested out before being released to the rest of the Marine Corps). I learned so much about so much, that it was hard to say I had a specialty. I did, however, find ways to stick to my Marine Corps roots while I was in.

Being that I wanted to experience the Marine Corps as much as the units I was attached to would let me experience it, I volunteered for a variety of things. My favorite was when I volunteered to be a range coach and was sent to PMI school to learn the fundamentals of primary marksmanship. Being a range coach taught me a lot of things, mostly how to utilize different teaching styles in order to effectively teach different types of people. It also taught me patience, and how to remain responsible for a large group's safety and well-being. Being a range coach also allowed me to interact with a variety of people I would never have had the chance of interacting with normally in my everyday job; Staff, officers, and other units mainly.

And to include my shameless plug, I proudly say that not one person left the range unqualified under my instruction.

But as time passes on in the service, the more knowledgeable and responsible individuals become crew chiefs and section leaders, and over time—I became both. I was the crew chief of four different systems and a test system, and the NCOIC in two different shops. What this ultimately means is that people trusted me to get what needed to get done, done. I had to answer to my supervisor and their supervisors, and I was accountable for not only the systems I worked on, but also the people who worked on them with me; from knowledge of our job, to making sure their clothes were serviceable and that they were brushing their teeth. It wasn't always fun, and definitely wasn't always rewarding, but because I had gotten to know so many people on the range (on a personal level), things got easier for me around the Marine Corps, which made things easier for the Marines in my shop as well.

(Fill in the rank) Graves became a name you could trust... for the most part.

Needless to say, once I got out of the Marine Corps I swore to Chesty Puller that I would never touch another multi-meter again. The fun of fixing problems had gotten far from reach for me, and when the time came to separate from the Corps, I was ready to leave all that behind me and find something new.

I learned quickly that companies were seeking out vets, and wanted us as bad as we needed a job. You have to understand that whether you serve two years or twenty, your knowledge on your specific trade surpasses any graduate fresh out of college. Our hands-on experience is qualification enough, and sometimes trumps 4 to 6-year degrees at some companies. So as bad as I wanted to do something else for money, the real money was once again falling back into my military trade: a radar technician.

The reality was, I was good at it. I was also resourceful, a self-starter, a quick learner, flexible, polite, well mannered—I could take orders, and give them as well. Sound familiar? In my new job I could travel freely from country to country, actually getting to experience the countries I visited without restrictions or rules set by my command. I could actually fix gear without fifteen other people around me, just taking up space, or officers constantly asking me when the systems will be operational again.

What I thought would be a waste of time on the outside, became my bread and butter.

The same could very well be similar for you. As much as I understand the feeling of wanting to leave the military in your rear-view mirror, you put in the time, and for some of you—literal blood, sweat, and tears into your trades. You've gone through situations most people will *never* experience, and that makes you a seasoned vet. Really think about whether or not you want to immediately start fresh with a brand new occupation, or find out if you mesh well with similar types of employment.

What you need to take away from this chapter is that if you take your job seriously while you're in the service, and actually learn your trade, you will already be ahead of the civilian working force. Your **O**n the **J**ob **T**raining is gold, whether it seems that way now or not. Many veterans will leave the service and learn something completely different. A lot of vets will find something similar to what they'd been doing while serving. Many might feel that they can't find a good paying job afterwards, and take whatever they feel they can get... but I assure you the job you're looking for is out there, and I will teach you where to look for them later on.

Remember: ***You made a sacrifice. You learned a trade. Your knowledge on that trade is gold <u>and can be monetized</u>.***

Don't Burn Bridges

Here's the timeline: You sign the dotted line at the recruiter's office and become a poolee. If your recruiter was awesome like mine, you may have had poolee functions where you were doing all that "crazy military stuff," like low crawling under jump ropes stretched out on orange cones in the sand, and doing pushups in freezing cold beach water at night. You do this for months before you ship, and brag to your friends about what a badass you're going to become, or already are since you've been "training like the real deal" already.

The day before all the poolee's ship out to their respective boot camps, you sit in MEPS and swear-in together, promising your life to your country and the men and women that live in it. Later, you jam into a bus off to boot camp and spend however many weeks your branch of service has you go through. But through the waking up at zero-dark-thirty, killing your body in a fashion that seems something that only the Spartan warriors would do, and having to do things in constant repetition because of the *one person* who *just can't get it*, you actually make it through boot camp—*proud* to have made it, and proud to have a title that so many heroes before you have had the honor of calling themselves. For some, that pride is short lived, but that's okay too.

For Marines, we had to go through Marine Combat Training (MCT), to learn how to breach buildings, shoot grenade launchers, and call in an airstrike. We also sat in the freezing cold night for hours at a time doing nothing but smoking cigarettes, chewing dip, and talking about our boot leave and what the Fleet is going to be like. After a few weeks of that, off to our occupational schools where we would then learn the basic aspects of our trade.

As you all well know, the students in your class become an extension of your family. You practically spend every waking hour with these same people, day in and day out. You learn your trade, you get hazed together, you drink, fight, pray and play. You may even visit their homes for holidays, and end up calling some other lady your mom. The bonds you build with the people you go to school with are long-term, and meaningful. It is here—where you start business networking, and you don't even know it yet.

Before I go any further, I know this is not the reality for *everybody*! I was in MOS school for well over a year, so I'd say the influence that your peers may have had on you might have a different affect. In fact, I know this to not be true for everyone, because I have conversations often with my best friend I went to boot camp with on how different our experiences were. For instance, I had some of my friends from MOS school in and at my wedding, whereas he keeps ZERO contact with any of his.

Professional Relationships

Let's be honest. There's absolutely no chance that you will get along with every single person you come across while serving in the military. You may become accustomed to their crap, and learn to deal with it, but you may never get to the point where you're getting beers together after work without some other friends around.

There was a guy in my MOS who we'd *known* was as racist as the Grand Dragon himself, and I ended up getting stationed in Okinawa with him. He had been there for four months before I had gotten there. The minute I got to my new shop I heard he'd gotten a Page 11 for hiding his black roommate's money, "to teach his nigger ass a lesson for leaving his dresser unlocked for field day inspection." That's right. Those were his actual words. I mean the dude had the largest confederate flag I'd ever seen hanging on his wall in the barracks, and I actually never knew that there were that many clothing items with the confederate flag print until I met him. His racism wasn't a secret.

But he broke. And before his tour in Oki was over, he'd had himself a few black friends who were patient enough to show him love and compassion. Isn't that the best thing about being in the service? Meeting people from all nooks and crannies of the country, learning how to interact with people who are different than yourself, and building a relationship strong enough that when placed in a combat situation, there is nothing you wouldn't do for those brothers and sisters to the left and right of you?

Don't get me wrong, I *hated* a few people—and I had my good reasons to. However, let me tell you this now... like any fraternity or sorority, when you leave the service, *these* are going to be the people who understand you the best. It is highly important to maintain good social standings with not only your peers from your military occupational schools, but all the service men and women, and civilian contractors you come in contact with throughout your enlistment; from your first duty station until it's time for you to separate from the service.

Believe it or not, the world *is* a small place, and the military is even smaller. These are all people you may run into again someday in *or* out of the service. As a civilian I've run into people I used to serve with in completely different countries, years after I'd seen them last. I've even run into people in passing at airports, and in random hotels while on vacation with my family.

Some people you run into may just *know* someone you served with or served under. When I separated and realized I needed to get work, I walked into a job fair that my first employer was holding, and I handed in my resume, took a seat, got through the first interview, and was asked to wait for a second interview.

Professional Relationships

As I sat in this room of hopeful future employees, I heard people talking about how hard it was to get into this company, and how this company is the best with benefits, camaraderie, and just making their employees feel like they have a home. Needless to say I was soaking it all in and hoping for the best. An older man in his late 40's and a goofy smile walks out and screams, "GRAVES!" I reply with a nice solid, "Yes'sir," and offered him a firm handshake. He introduced himself and then he said, "We may have a few things in common."

It turns out that even though this company dealt with a completely different type of radar than I was accustomed to, he and I shared the same MOS, except he hadn't been in the Marine Corps for well over 15 years. But he knew my first ever Master Sergeant—*very well in fact.* So much so, that they still meet up and have BBQ's with each other's families.

I had already had a foot in the door because of the two bonds—the first being the Marine brotherhood bond, the second being the military background bond. But now we had a mutual acquaintance in common, and you better believe he reached out to her and asked some questions about who I was as a person.

The people you encounter will always hold an image of who you are. That old saying, "a first impression is a lasting impression," holds very true. You may not have a lot of one-on-one time with everyone you come in contact with, so keep in mind that your attitude and your personality for those few moments in time define who you are to everyone you meet. If you meet someone once, and all they meet is the sarcastic and abrasive you, they will never get to understand that you were just having a bad day and that wasn't the real you. To them, you are rude and hard to deal with. To the guy who fell in a squadron run, and then you helped them up and dusted them off—you will forever be a good person to them, considering you never run into each other again.

Not burning bridges works in other ways too. If you establish great rapport with someone, a strong relationship—whether it be at work only, on a softball team, at the gym, in church, or wherever it is that you spend your time, those relationships can highly benefit you in the future if you maintain the proper connections.

If you've created a positive image of yourself to the right connections, people will keep you in mind. What happens when veterans get out is that they start to live a completely different life. Some jump into the trade they had left behind, like yours truly, and some go on to create their own businesses… and they're looking for like-minded individuals that they can rely upon to help run and grown their companies. They're looking for partners, and loyal friends that they can trust with their lives—and who better than you?

Soon when companies are looking for more employees that they can rely on, or if a friend is starting a business on their own and looking for someone they can trust—if you've done your job by networking properly you may be a top runner on someone's list. Soon, when *you* are looking for a job or applying to college, these are also the people you're going to be able to reach out to for references and referrals. This is the same way network groups work, it's how fraternities and sororities work, it's the same as church groups and other groups like the Free Masons work. They keep their own in mind first! So it's very important that you create and maintain an image of yourself you want to professionally market, and maintain open communication often with people you've established any type of relationship with.

I know for a fact, that if something happened to me and I needed a job, a place to live, or even an ear to talk to—I have options. That is the feeling that you want to have when you walk away from the military—that you will be okay, and not be alone to fend for yourself. If you keep your bridges intact, you will be able to walk across them at any time for whatever it is you need. Essentially, It was me not having burned bridges during my enlistment that ultimately helped me get hired into my first job out of the Marine Corps, and also in my court martial… but that's another chapter.

Remember: *There is no work like <u>Network</u>. Every interaction in the military could possibly change your life later down the road. Whether you realize it or not, a little genuine kindness and respect can go a long way. Do whatever it takes to not burn bridges in your life.*

ACRONYMS

Before my wife and I started dating, she was a recruiter for a staffing company that was looking for tech nerds like myself. And when she took her first look at my resume, she simply handed it back to me and said, "you can't have these acronyms on here. People don't know what this means outside the military."

Are you seriously telling me that civilians won't understand what DOD, AIRCOM, MOS, OPS, MEU, BEQ, AFN, or ADCOMSUBORDCOMPHIBSPAC stand for? (That last one is real, look it up). In order to be taken seriously in the hiring process, I had to learn how to write a resume correctly.

The Transitional Assistance Management Program and the Transition Assistance program (TAMP/TAPS) classes that are required for us to attend prior to separating from the service does a pretty good job at explaining and going over basic resumes. However, it was hard to remember what was said to me about the specifics of writing a resume while I was sitting in a class trying to wrap my head around the fact that in just a few weeks I would be a civilian. So I'd forgotten whether or not if acronyms were absolutely necessary on my resume—and that was my issue.

The answer was no, they are not necessary for *most* jobs. However, if you're applying to an employer who you know is keen to the verbiage of your military job, then use the acronyms for that specific company only, and only after you have spelled them out first.

Know your audience.

If you're applying to be the director of human resources at Disneyland, they can care less that you "Maintained and repaired four airfield RADAR systems. Including, but not limited to: the AN/TPS-59 (V3), AN/TPS-63, AN/MPQ-64, Sentinel, and all sub-assemblies including but not limited to the KIT, KIR, AN/MPQ- 62, AN/UPX-27, AN/UPX-37, and the AN/ UPX-60 identification friend or foe and fiber optics." Instead, they want to know in laymen's terms what makes you qualified for *their* position you're applying for.

KNOW. YOUR. AUDIENCE.

Here's how to create a great resume before you even actually think about creating a resume.

Note number one: Any, and I mean *any* projects you work on—whether it be helping a different shop or unit lay fiber optic cable while deployed in the Philippines, or providing assistance in the logistical aspects of some joint military exercise from your home base, create a file on your computer and note it. Note it not only so you can get used to keeping track of your activities for your FITREP (when you get to that level of evaluation), but also so you can incorporate it into your civilian resume. *"Laid fiber optic cable for communications systems centers,"* or, *"Provided logistical assistance in Talon Vision,"* reads much better than, "*Went to Korea and supported missions.*"

Make a *Master Resume* of some sort. I learned about this in TAMP/TAPS but I wish I had done it sooner than this class. It is not a real resume, just a really big rough draft for you to pick and choose from. Essentially a master resume will be that list that you are annotating the projects you are working on as you continue throughout your military career. From this master resume, you'll be able to tailor a resume for whatever job you're looking for. For example, while I was looking for a job, I created two separate resumes; one for the tech side, and one for a management role.

A sample of my Master Resume looked like this:
- Repaired the electronic sub-systems that kept the main operating systems on-line
- Managed a small group of 12 people for a leadership project put together to reduce impact of Fiscal Year (FY) losses
- Maintained Hazardous Material Data Sheet (MSDS) as the Safety manager of my shop
- Became Third Echelon Test Set (TETS) certified Jan 2004

- Completed a HMMWV driving certification course
- Created a training program for weekly safety briefs for a group of 30 individuals.
- Completed Primary Marksmanship instructor course (8531)
- Received Joint Meritorious Unit Commendation award (JMUC) April 2004

So looking at this sample master resume, you can see how we would filter through for what we would like to see on a tailored resume for a technical job, and what we would possibly only use for something specific for a managerial role.

Once you've figured out what it is you want on your resume, highlight your best qualifications in a brief paragraph about yourself, *really* selling yourself. Let them know that you're a military veteran with however many years, you have under your belt, and tell them what you bring to the table. What makes you stand out compared to those guys who have been formally trained by UCLA or ITT Tech? Reinforce that because of your military background, you *are* a self-motivator, and understand the importance of teamwork and mission accomplishment. Highlight <u>**QUALITY OVER QUANTITY**</u>! Utilize the same type of verbiage you would hear for someone receiving yet *another* Navy Achievement Medal for handing out mail at the mailroom...*somebody* figured out how to make that job sound glorious enough for medal recognition.

Do the same for your resume.

Finally, when it comes to interviewing, remember: leave the acronyms in the military unless the person directly in front of you is knowledgeable on what it is you're talking about; meaning—the company you're interviewing with is inline with the job you had in the military. When you have the opportunity to sit in front of a hiring manager, or anyone in a position to pass you on to the next level of interviewing, *know your audience.*

Using the Disneyland human resource example again, once you're asked to come in for an interview, speak to the person across from you with the respect that you would give a Commanding Officer, but *break down* what it was you did in the service like you would do to a classroom full of high school seniors. Be clear and concise. Learn how to read people's faces for any type of confusion that may need clarification, and most importantly— remain calm. You know what you know, and it's not important to force yourself or the job you had to sound more complicated than it already was.

Remember: *KNOW YOUR AUDIENCE! Make yourself clear and concise on what it is you offer. Think like the individuals working at the job you want, and fulfill the needs of the positions you're seeking. This is no time to be humble, writing a resume is a battle of the best and most qualified.*

HOW TO GROW A BEARD

JOIN A SMALL GROUP

Because of the constant fighting in legislation and the news you may hear about or read in the media, it may sometimes seem like the government doesn't protect it's veterans. However, take it from me—the government doesn't just kick you out of the gun club and then make us fend for ourselves.

Over time you may hear about all kinds of programs that veterans are qualified for, or help they can receive. The number of things we have access to when we get out is incredible; you just have to do the groundwork to find out *everything* that's out there.

So how do we know what's available for us? Easy! Besides flipping through the vast information you should receive in the TAMP/TAP classes, you have the glorious Internet.

If you're unsure how anything works, such as the VA loan, search "VA loans in my state." Even Navy Federal or your local bank will have the information about those types of loans. Looking to open up your own bar, tattoo shop, or candle store? Do a little online research to help guide you to the best veteran specific low rate option loan. Know that there are perks and pluses to bc a veteran-ran business. Know that you are not left out there to figure it all out for yourself.

When I separated, I walked into the Greater Los Angles VA to register with them. I didn't know what to expect, or why I was registering at all, but I felt it would be something that should be done. You see, I had questions about some legal issues that I was still unsure of how it would effect my civilian life, and I also needed to get set up with physical therapy, or at least see what my options for healthcare were.

The VA's general office initiated my claims for removing my ex from my records, initiated my claims for disability, guided me in the right direction for how to work the Post 9/11 G.I. Bill, and even sought out to locate my medical records because of a change in plans for where my home of record was going to be. They also recommended that I register with a smaller organization that would be willing to take lead on any type of paperwork that may get sent back to me and I may need help with, and so I registered with the DAV.

The Disabled American Veterans group is a smaller group that acts like a small law firm for you, and provides you with any and all information that you'll need to start out, or at least point you in the right direction. Other groups like the Veterans of Foreign Wars (VFW), or American Veterans (AMVETS), The American Legion, Wounded Warriors Project, Paralyzed Veterans of America, Purple Heart Foundation and many more, offer their time and services to help rehabilitate the men and women who served. Some are even very well prepared to help the families in need as well.

Did you know, that if you died today (God forbid), that your burial services would be taken care of completely if your family requested it through the VA, or rather, contacted a smaller veteran group to start the process for you? Small things like that save families thousands of dollars during an already unfortunate time of grieving. And the smaller groups have more time than the VA has, in order to talk to you about these hidden gems, and ability to lead you in the right direction... not to mention they are *much* easier to get a hold of.

Here's a little tip from the wise. When you call the VA for something, expect to be hung up on, redirected to someone that will never ever be able to help you, get redirected to the main menu a few times, oh... and be hung up on. It's very hard to make a simple call for a simple question. I once called the VA to ask a question about an education claim I had as I was leaving my house. During the whole time I was on hold, I drove to the VA, signed in, and had my name called to be seen—all before I hung up from being on hold for that whole time period (I admit I had a lot of time on my hands that day).

Utilize the smaller groups! They offer the same assistance, but are more accessible. Most have some type of requirement you must meet in order to qualify to become a member, but I'm sure the majority of people who serve today meet the criteria for most of the groups. Even groups like the Purple Heart Foundation only ask that you are a veteran and/or family of a veteran, regardless if you have a Purple Heart or not. These groups are here to protect the vet. Use them.

So what did I pull from my small group, the DAV? What can the groups help you with as a veteran on the outside of the service?

EDUCATION. This almost seems like a no-brainer, but sincerely pay attention to whether or not you want to use the G.I. Bill or the Post 9/11 G.I. Bill. You can switch from the normal bill (Chapter 30) to the Post 9/11 (Chapter 33) but you can't switch back. More on that later.

PURCHASING A HOUSE. This like the education benefits, seem like the obvious benefits. In fact most servicemen and women are looking to utilize these two benefits immediately on day one of becoming Mr. or Ms./Mrs. Schmuckatelli.

MEDICAL COMPENSATION. This is what I hear most from guys getting out, "I'm not going to use the tax payers money for some shit that I hurt being stupid during deployment. I'm not a bitch." Then I meet retired 50-year-old Master Gunnery Sergeants and retired Navy Chiefs who've been out for God knows how long, and they want to know what I know about claiming a disability.

You see, we've been bred as military personal to be tough, and suck it up. Our doses of Motrin and water have created a mean green, war-fighting machine that's invincible and tougher than any civilian to walk the face of the planet. And as much as that may all be true, the truth is, as you get older, and more in tune with your civilian self, your body will start to show you who's boss and not vice-versa.

By no means am I saying to abuse the system. That is as far from the message as possible. But if you have a service-related injury, make sure you have it noted in your medical records. It's okay to be a hard-ass when you're young, single, and don't have many obligations besides the one you signed up for. But when you're 30 or 40 with a kid and you have to get shoulder surgery because of an old Marine Corps injury you sucked up for the last 11 years, you deserve to receive the best care possible.

VOCREHAB. Now to get into some of the more uncommon knowledge. VocRehab is a program designed to help service connected disabled vets learn a *new trade* or get certified or licensed in something they have been pursuing but are close to/or have run out of money for. For those individuals having a hard time seeking employment on their own, the VocRehab office is also able to seek out employment to place vets in programs like Veterans Opportunity to Work (VOW).

What most people don't know about VocRehab is that you can utilize it in conjunction with the GI bill if you know you're going to run out of benefits before you finish your degree. There are certain cases, assuming you have not completely run out of education benefits, that VocRehab will step in and pay for up to a year of your tuition as well as the living stipend. But remember, you must be enrolled as a full time student while working a degree plan.

Now, you *can* apply to VocRehab as a non-service connected vet, but the chance of those individuals getting selected is slim. Don't let that derail your effort to utilize the benefit, because *every single case* is a case-by-case basis whether you're service connected or not.

MILITARY ONE SOURCE. *www.militaryonesource.mil* is pretty much a one-stop-shop for questions and answers. No, they didn't pay me to say this, and I have zero affiliation with them. But whenever I have had a friend or co-worker ask me about something I'm unsure of, I can either find it on the VA's website through a lot of clicking and searching, or I come here.

Life insurance, pension for those 65 and older and in real need of help, grants and loans for veterans specifically, business loans, low rate personal loans... even knowing about smaller benefits like specific Chase branches that offer vets a free safety deposit box, perks at theme parks such as discounted Disneyland packages, or the ability to receive 10% off your purchases at Lowe's and Home Depot—these are all things that you qualify for, because you're a veteran. And they are just some of the benefits that you find out from the smaller groups, since it's the smaller groups that tend to advertise opportunities to us that the VA normally wouldn't.

The last piece of information about smaller groups that I'd like to pass on to you is that it is imperative to be very cautious about who's reaching out their hands to help you. There are many companies that will magically get your name, address, or even your phone number, and start asking you for some type of interest in what they're selling. Normally this is true when you've bought a house or applied for some type of financial loan. Before you sign papers and agree to anything make sure that the organization is credible and that you aren't going to be taken through the ringer. Do your research. Call the company you want to do business with and ask some very detailed questions. But also do yourself a favor and call a small group like the DAV or AMVETS to see if the company you're about to do business with is on a flag list of people taking advantage of vets. This isn't paranoia... its precaution.

Remember: *You served your country. You put yourself out there for a possibility to lose your life by someone who thinks you are the root of all evil. Even if you haven't taken a bullet for the cause, you were brave enough to take the chance. You've given to the country—take this time and let the country give back to you. Find a group that's going to help you through the process of the rest of your life.*

KNOW YOUR WORTH

I mentioned while talking about benefits to make sure nobody is taking advantage of you. Let me share with you something that's taken me a long time to figure out.

You see, how the military is structured, we're not paid much. That's no secret. Yes, we're given COLA and/or Per Diem (depending on where you are stationed), housing, medical, dental, clothing allowance, etc... but even when all that is added up, the average second term enlisted individual my age, while I served, was only making $27,516-$33,016 a year. It didn't matter if you made scrambled eggs for your whole career or if you had to get FAA certified to guide and land aircraft, if you both were the same rank who'd been in around the same amount of time—you were getting the same pay. So you can see how confusing that makes life for those of us transitioning out into the civilian world.

Most of us don't know our worth.

We were never taught that. We assume that anything over $27,516 is a gift from God, and so what happens is, companies will prey on veterans when it comes to salary.

Imagine being a company who is going to hire an electrician. You know as a company, if you want a *quality* electrician who can fix anything and do it properly, you're going to have to pay close to the higher end of the salary cap, which right now is in the $30/hr range. But someone who just got out of the military who has the same qualifications, knows and performs the same type of job as good if not better, and is looking to be an electrician at your company but is willing to take whatever you'll give him (since this will most likely be his first job and all)... that veteran is going to make money on the low end of $13.57/hr, or closer to the median price of $20/hr.

$20 an hour sounds like Fort Knox to a guy who had just been telling dick jokes to his friends over beers in the barracks, and depending on where you're living, it might be more than enough. But let me put it into this perspective: There are minimum wage earners protesting as I speak to have minimum wage raised to $15 an hour, or $28,800 a year.

So for your training, and your hands-on knowledge, and your specialty knowledge on specific pieces of equipment, and your work ethic, attitude, not to mention *years* of high stress situation experience in your trade and professionalism—which essentially should be included in that monetary package—companies will never pay you what you're worth, if you allow it to happen.

When I got out the Marine Corps, a buddy of mine allowed me to sleep on his couch until I got a job and back on my feet. It's a shitty feeling being a burden in someone's home for more than a week, even worse, a few months... but when you have good friends, especially those who are also vets, it makes life a little easier.

Knowing that I needed to get off that couch, I immediately started looking for a job. I'm not trying to be funny with words but looking for a job *is* a full time job. With all the researching of companies I went through to see if I was a right fit for them and vice-versa, with all the constant modifying of cover letters to hiring managers, and going out on job interviews in different cities, while trying to pick up work to kick back to my buddy for couch rental and put food in my mouth—the feeling of overwhelming stress took over.

I had gone to *so* many job interviews, and at times had nobody calling me back, and just as equally I had people calling me back offering me jobs for $30-40K. I turned down each and every offer that wasn't in the $50K margin. I didn't know what I was worth then, but I knew it was more than $50K. I mean, I was essentially an engineer.

My couch-landlord would constantly get on my case for turning all the job offers down. In fact often he'd say, "You gotta take whatever's being offered to you. There are no jobs, you are being fucking stupid right now. Take what you can get and stop being so fucking picky." We had a lot of these conversations, but I stood my ground and I believed whole-heartedly that I was worth *something* in the $50K range.

Desperation of the long search was wearing thin on my soul, and I was being held up on a hope that a very well-known electronics company was going to hire me as a medical equipment installer, specifically installing MRI and CT Scan machines. I'd interviewed with many individuals on their staff to keep me interested, and had even had lunch with the Southern California manager. But by law they had to interview all that applied for this position… so I was told. While waiting for that company to pull the trigger on me, I received a call from a company I'd forgotten I'd twice interviewed with.

This company's HR manager fed me all the right things over the phone; competitive salary, vacation days, travel 25% of the time, paid overtime, 401K <u>and</u> a pension, room to grow at my own pace… and no talk about money. I'd asked if I could have until Friday to think about it, (being that I was also told from the well-known electronics company that they'd let me know as late as Friday afternoon if they'd be offering me a position with their company), the HR manager simply said, "no, take it or leave it."

I took it.

I was desperate to have a job at that point, I was extremely tired of all the interviews and searching, I was over trying to sell myself. And if I've ever learned anything in life—it's that there are no guarantees in life. So there was no guarantee that the electronics company was going to call me back with positive news.

Plus *"take it or leave it"* is kind of bully-ish.

When I showed up for that position, I asked when we were going to talk about salary. That same HR manager simply told me, there is no salary negotiation, "we're going to pay you this amount, and you can take that, or leave it as well." It was in my range, and I couldn't complain. So once again I took it.

As life went on, I did very good work for this company, often getting recognized with a small $100 bonus check, or even a rare $600 bonus check, but those slowed down... and not just for me, but company wide. I'd been praised, sought out for jobs internally, and requested by external customers to come work on their systems.

And then one day, lightning struck. Me and another Marine buddy of mine, in my specialized group of engineers, were "promoted" two-whole pay grades—with no pay. Simply because they felt like we should be on the same job title level as some of the senior guys, being that we were doing similar work.

There was no way that he or I could get to a salary that would ever be fair to us, because we weren't allowed to grow on the pay scale and there was nowhere left for us to go or grow. Imagine it like this; it would be like if a Sergeant was promoted to Sergeant Major today with no pay increase, and the only other job above him is Sgt. Major of the Marine Corps.

I bitched about it, yes. It was unfair. At that point I'd given three years of solid work to a company and had only seen a $0.40 increase in my salary, only to be promoted twice with no salary increase. I started calling around to my friends who held similar jobs, and found that some were making well over $100K, and some started out at $70K. I knew then that I had been robbed of what I was worth.

I find that out here in the civilian world, vets are usually loyal to the companies that pick them up right after the service; until those same vets start to see that they're being taken for granted, and often taken advantage of. Once you start to see how much you're worth, a different type of fire burns in you and you either become bitter or motivated for change depending on your situation.

So how do you find out what you're worth?

Well a quick Internet search of your trade or trades that require similar skills will give you a ball park figure from low to high. How you decipher where

you should be on the pay scale is by truthfully asking yourself how valuable you are:
- Do you have special certifications that make you stand out from individuals just coming out of school, like IEEE, or any type of CompTIA certification program?
- Did you go through any type of apprentice, journeyman, or master programs in your trade?
- Do you have a clearance?
- Do you have to be certified through government-standardized certifications like OSHA?
- How in depth do you know your job?
- Have you managed, or trained others?

All these things, which should be noted on your resume, are grounds for higher pay!

Even if you were forced to get certified as a young enlisted or officer, those certifications really do mean something in the working world. *Every skill you have* translates. Certain computer programs that you utilized on a daily basis, translate. Anything that you had to learn for your job in the military translates.

Another reliable way to find out what the civilian world is offering your trade is to talk to a civilian counterpart. Most jobs in the service have a civilian counterpart that we either order spare parts from or work with hand-in-hand in the field, or on a daily basis. Since the military doesn't actually fabricate it's own equipment, there are hundreds of contractors that we could possibly reach out to with a little curiosity. If you ask your tech rep what a fair salary is, I'm sure they'd not only be willing to tell you a decent salary to settle for, or even recommend what you should shoot for, but they might even help you get a foot in the door. Lastly, see if your civilian counterparts will write you a letter of recommendation if you're applying for a job within their company or field.

It took me close to five years to gain courage to admit how over-worked, and under-appreciated not only myself was, but the small group of specialized engineers that I worked with and have built family-bonded relationships with. Don't get me wrong, you live and you learn, so I can't be upset at all. I love where I am today, and I wouldn't be here if it weren't for the journey I had to take to get here—but if I can help just one person not have to suffer this lesson, I'll have done my job.

Remember: ***KNOW YOUR WORTH!*** *People may seek out to hire vets, but most of the time it benefits them more than it benefits you. Be strong and ask the questions you need to know before accepting a job, and don't be strong-armed into anything. Believe it or not, contrary to what people are saying out there, there are jobs if you're willing to get out your comfort zone.*

How to Find a Job That's Right for You

The first call I received about a job was from an insurance sales company who had sought *me* out. I hadn't called or reached out to insurance agencies, so this was exciting because I thought I was special, I thought I was needed.

I was excited. My girlfriend was excited. It was my first interview, and I was going to knock it out of the park. I shaved my face for the first time in 4 months since I'd been out, I got a nice fresh haircut. I made sure all the loose strings on my 3-piece suit were snipped off, and my shoes we nice and buffed out. I even bought a nice binder to hold my resumes and a pen.

I looked sharp.

As I drove myself to one of the nicest parts of Los Angeles, and walked up to this huge corporate building, I made one last *wish-me-good-luck* text to my girlfriend, took a few deep breaths, and then went to show these people what this hard-charging Marine can bring to the table. I took the elevator up to one of the top floors, and as I got off I could see miles and miles of Los Angeles—all the way down to the beach. I was instantly impressed with this company that had wanted me to come interview for them.

I sat with a young guy; maybe 23 years old at his oldest, and answered each of his questions, trying to read the impression I was giving to him by studying his facial expressions as I answered each one. As far as I could tell—he loved me. He gave me some positive feedback and told me to wait for the next round, and that he was excited for the possibility of working with me. I was eating this all up. I'd known I had knocked the interview out of the park!

A slightly older gentleman, probably 27 years old, came to get me and asked me to wait in the room for a indoctrination video… if I was interested. Now I wouldn't say at this point I was interested, but I was definitely curious. So I did. I waited in that room with one other person. Then two. Then five. That room filled up with thirteen more people, and then I realized—this company would take anybody willing because it was basically a sales force pyramid scheme. I'd been had! I'd watched that video out of politeness, but was incredibly broken inside.

What's funny is that I know a few other vets who got a similar opportunity as their first interview at other companies—and I can't lie, it was disheartening.

That experience gave me the insight that I needed to be particularly selective in what it was I would say yes to an interview for. It made me very cautious to what I was applying to. But even after a few weeks of hitting the job search pretty hard, I wasn't receiving calls back. That was discouraging in itself. It was then that my girlfriend, the nerd recruiter as I called her, asked me if I had a LinkedIn profile. Being that I just figured out what Facebook was a year or two before that, the answer was no.

I'm sure it's not a known secret now—what LinkedIn is, but in case you actually don't know, LinkedIn is a networking site strictly for professionals. Any profession really, but essentially it is a professional Facebook. So I created an account. Nothing really happened from it, so I'd told her some days later after she'd asked me again if I created a profile that, "I didn't see the point." She then explained how it worked.

Essentially it's like a online resume. You fill in the information as accurate and complete as you can, and then the secret is having a solid introduction, and belonging to groups you're interested in being seen by. The introduction should be similar to your summary on your resume—short and enticing. The groups however, should be tailored to:
    1) What type of job you're looking for
    2) Which companies you're interested in
    3) Hobbies you may have
    4) Military groups specific to you

WHAT TYPE OF JOB ARE YOU LOOKING FOR? The groups you sign up for should be in your realm of interest. I joined random engineering groups, avionics groups, field service engineering groups, and other techie stuff. If you're looking to become a fire fighter or a police officer in a specific area, join groups tailored to the city or government jobs, specific firehouses or police departments.

You could also type in something general like *event planner*, *advertising professionals*, or *money*, and a list of businesses and groups that fall into category will pop up, giving you the opportunity to connect with them, and start networking.

There are even prep groups you can search for, that would help with questions or training regiments to prepare you for future interviews. Whatever the job is you're looking for, I'm willing to bet there's a group created to support that group.

WHAT COMPANIES ARE YOU INTERESTED IN? Also, what companies would you want interested in you? LinkedIn is a two way street; as you're looking for employment, recruiters and HR reps will look for individuals that are looking for employment and are qualified for positions they have open. Via LinkedIn, they can see whom you know that they know, and reach out and get a feel of who it is you are before you even know you're going to apply to their company. That's why it's important to make sure you get into the company's LinkedIn group. If you want to work for Lockheed or Sensis, join their group or follow their company pages. If you'd like to work in a non-profit, like the Ronald McDonald

Foundation or the Multiple Sclerosis Society—join their group.

By joining groups, you're not only showing and displaying interest, but you get to be caught up on new information, upcoming job fairs, open positions, new management changes, and many other things that companies decide to update LinkedIn with.

WHAT ARE YOUR HOBBIES? If you went onto my LinkedIn profile you'd see a few Diving groups and Volleyball groups that I've joined. Keep in mind, when you share a common interest with someone, it's easier to gain rapport with those people. When you utilize the hobby groups as a part of your professional platform, you are networking with other professionals whom you may not have been able to from other groups that you've joined.

For example, say you wanted to be some type of director or a manager of some sort, and you just aren't having any luck. On LinkedIn, post in your hobby group that you're *a veteran who has just separated from the (branch of service) with (type of experience), and is looking for (type of work). If any of you fellow (hobby enthusiasts) are looking for, or knows anyone looking for a hard-working veteran to join their team, please message me and I will happily send over a resume. Have a wonderful day!*

Don't overlook the power of the common interest! You'll find you can really get into a lot of interesting situations and maybe some random event you never knew existed by joining your hobby groups.

JOIN THE MILITARY GROUPS. While you were in the service, you may have felt like people weren't really watching out for you and could care less about you. On the outside, it's polar opposite. Vets take care of vets. So every possible Military group that you qualify for—join.

Here are a few that I'm personally a part of:
- U.S. Veteran
- US Military Veterans Network
- Hire Military
- Marine Corps Professionals
- Marine Vets – MarineVets.com
- ViaVet
- Defense and Aerospace Connections
- U.S. Government Connections

Other groups I'm a part of are specifically Marine Corps groups, Unit groups, or Government job groups. I also requested to join a lot of groups that require a security clearance. These groups require you to have a clearance, some as low as Confidential (which the majority of the military falls into). Join them anyway, because if you're qualified for a job listing and they really want you, some companies _will_ pay for your clearance.

Some of those groups to join are:
- ClearedJobs.com
- Cleared Connections
- US Security Clearance Careers
- Security Clearance Jobs
- US Government Security Clearance
- Security Cleared Jobs.com for DV, SC & NATO jobs

These groups are all networking groups, and posting to the group individually makes sure that the members of the group, as well as recruiters and HR personnel, see what it is you're selling. Understand this, the people in those groups only see your post if you post into the group. That means make sure that the same intro you wrote into the hobby groups, you post into these individual groups as well.

Once my girlfriend taught me the way LinkedIn worked, and I utilized it just like I'd told you, messages and emails were filling my inbox at an astronomical rate. I essentially found my first job in this manner when I'd received a LinkedIn message about their job fair starting two hours from when I received the message.

Besides using job searching sites like Monster, Careerbuilder, Indeed, SimplyHired, or whatever else pops up on the World Wide Web, other ways you can find jobs are by getting in with staffing recruiters. Recruiters are individuals who are looking to staff other companies by searching for quality candidates. What happens is that a company's HR is too busy to man the daily routines of dealing with the employee's *and* looking for quality individuals to join the team. So they outsource that part of the process and do the final hiring interview.

There are two staffing companies that I personally worked with and recommend to anyone in the tech fields when they get out: *Lucas Group*, and *Orion International.* Both seek out jobs for technical veterans. Other staffing agencies such as *Volt Military*, *Aerotek*, *Bradley-Morris Cameron-Brooks,* and *Maxim Government Services* are reputable companies too, dedicated to find veterans jobs, and all may provide a few different companies on their hiring list that others don't.

I can't tell you how I came across these two companies I used, maybe it was a search I did on the Internet, but I'll tell you what, this is where you need to turn to for the *maximum exposure* and *guaranteed* interviews.

How these companies work is that they give you a rep that works for you. Your rep finds out what it is you're good at—your strengths and weaknesses, and then they invite you to a hotel, or conference hall to learn how to interview. They then send you off to sell yourself to a number of companies who they've brought to the hotel or conference hall to meet you... and forty other possible candidates.

The thing is, you all won't meet with the same companies so the competition does thin out a bit.

My first meeting with Lucas Group was overwhelming to say the least. I was asked my preferences of whom I wanted to interview with; companies like Intel, Boeing, and Toshiba had been there, along with some smaller names that were also on the market for vets. Some of the companies would hold a Q&A with a larger group before diving into interviews in order to weed out those who were just on the fence of whether or not they wanted to interview. Everyone here was just as eager to get a great job as I was.

I met with four companies that morning, and I had great interviews. I even had a few callbacks, but the best thing that I took from that first meeting was learning how to interview. Now I had already known how to interview from previous employment I had before I left to the Marine Corps, but as a technical man looking for a technical job, the interviews were a little more… technical. And so I prepared for the next round.

The only thing I really recommend; if you go this route and you strongly feel like you want to interview with a specific company and that company is not on your interview schedule that is assigned to you—speak up! Say something and stand your ground if you have to with the recruiting company's representatives. The reason I say this is because I desperately wanted to interview with that well-known electronics company I had mentioned earlier that was going to hire me as an MRI and CT Scan equipment installer, but that company wasn't on my interview schedule. Early in the morning, I had asked for the opportunity to interview with them, and then was blown off. I asked and asked again later, and was blown off again. At the end of the interview day—as the companies were wrapping up, I almost demanded that I be taken seriously about getting me in an interview with them.

The rep didn't think I would have been a good fit, that's why he didn't want me interviewing. But I owned that interview—and not only was I a good fit, I ended up being the lead runner for that job, and if you remember from the previous chapter I'd mentioned this story in, I'd met with multiple managers, including the manager of the Southern California region, but time wasn't on my side.

Now I didn't find my job through Lucas Group or Orion, but they prepared me for other interviews. They have a lot to offer and if you're wiling to move from your hometown, across the country or even the world, the possibilities of employment are endless. **AND IF AT ANYTIME** a staffing agency asks you for money—dump them. There shouldn't be one person asking you for money, because *they* get paid from the hiring company.

It is also important to note that when you are working with a recruiting agency, some positions may be on a temporary to permanent basis, or may even be on a contract (meaning you're guaranteed x-amount of time, and may be renewed if the position is still needed, or can be funded). Many contracts turn permanent, and it is an excellent way to get your foot in the door of a specific company and gain experience for your resume. Some recruiting companies may even offer benefits if you are on a contract, long-term employment, or an open-ended contract option. It's important to ask about what your options are when you have the opportunity to.

One last thing you should look into is keeping an eye out for job fairs, especially veteran specific job fairs. You often get notices like these from emails from the small groups like AMVETS, DAV, or the American Legion. Single companies like Kaiser Permanente may hold them, or a large multi-corporation job fair might be set up at a convention center. Keep an eye out for them.

Oh, I almost forgot! For all of you who still have your old email address that read aNgLeEyEs69@netgear.com, 2Big2BUrs@prodigy.com, or whatever you are holding onto from sixth grade—it's time for an upgrade.

In today's world, email addresses are in fact, your first impression when sending in your resumes to businesses. If a potential employer gets your resume from BooBooMagooTwo22@yahoo.com, that may in fact be the last thing they find out about you. Do yourself a favor and create a nice simple professional email that you will use to do all your adult correspondence with. Something with your full name or initials, something simple and plain, and let your personality stand out on its own when it's time to meet you in person.

I understand that knowing what it is you really want to do when you get out is hard to figure out. Unless you loved your job in the service, you may not know what it is that you're seeking out for yourself. A lot of the military skills you learned in your trade, or in general, are all marketable. Sometimes with a little creativity, you can tailor a resume to fit your dream job. Whatever the situation, you might find it useful to carry around a copy of your resume on a thumb drive attached to your keychain just in case opportunity knocks and is looking for you.

Hunting for the right job is hard work, but in the end it is in fact rewarding. Don't wait until you EAS to start looking for a job. It took me four solid moths, of 30-40 hour proactive weeks, to land my first job. Use these tools as early as six months or earlier before you separate from the service. It's not necessary to settle for a job, if you start searching early enough, and the earlier you start looking for a job, the less of a chance you take the first thing that is thrown your way once you've become a civilian.

Remember: *There are jobs out there for all of us. It's up to us to utilize every tool available to us in order to maximize our options for a job that we will enjoy going to everyday.*

How to Grow a Beard

Wrapping up Loose Ends

EAS'ing is kind of like packing up for a vacation. A really long and much needed vacation. But just like packing up for a vacation, you're going to have that feeling that something just isn't right. You are bound to have that feeling like you have forgotten something really important.

Most likely you're going to be right.

Besides the checklist that your unit should give you telling you where you need to check out of (organized by the months, weeks, and days prior to separating, who you need to speak to, and appointments you need to make), and the TAMP/TAP list of chores you should get done before you EAS… make sure you don't forget about the more personal things, like finishing the things you've started or making sure you have a way to finish them.

One of my personal loose ends was college. I didn't know if I was going to continue, or if I'd transfer, but I did <u>zero</u> research when it came to what I was going to do with my credits as well as what my options were. Fortunately for me, I had already started college, and finished my Associate Degree—so some of the bigger things were already done.

Something you may want to make sure you have situated is your JST/SMART transcript. The Joint Service Transcript or once known as the Sailor-Marine American Counsel on Education Registry Transcript, is a complicated way to say free college credit. That's right, all the small little trainings, exercises, qualifications, certifications, and career courses you've ever taken (voluntarily or not), get turned into American Counsel on Education (ACE) credits. But you've got to be on top of this. Make sure all of your classes, or any type of extra educational military education (like MCI's) are accounted for—whether you get credit for them or not.

Being that I've gone to college while both in the service and out of the service, I know what can and has happened to fellow veterans. Each and every school should have a veterans administration that should know all these answers, but take it from me, do not rely solely on them. They **should** know, and some will know all of the answers to your questions, but sometimes the college's veteran personnel aren't always in sync with new rule changes, different school programs, or even in sync with each other.

Before you EAS, whether or not you're going to attend college right away or never, request a JST/SMART transcript for the sake of having it just in case. Also, if you are in school, ask for an unofficial and at least two *official* transcripts. You won't need to do anything after this point, but keep them close to your DD-214.

These items essentially are not hard to get, but simply a hassle if you don't have any handy and you're trying to make a last minute push into a university. Also, if you're planning on enrolling in college and haven't done so yet, do yourself the favor of taking college entry exams such as the SAT, GRE, ACT, GMAT, LSAT, MCAT, or any other aronym'd placement exam out there you that might need for the colleges that you may be interested in applying to. Those tests are free to take on base, and if you fail you can continue to take them without wasting your own money.

Last bit of college tip advice I have, is to CLEP the courses you believe you can pass so you don't have to take the classes themselves. The College Level Examination Program (CLEP) exams, are tests created to test your knowledge on any given subject—from basic English comprehension to Pre-Calculus. Once they have been passed, they will give you ACE accreditation for most schools you would apply to. As long as they're free for you while on active duty, there is no harm/no foul for taking them just to see if you can pass them and knock some college credits off your transcript. Any school issues you have going on besides that, tie up those loose ends.

Another loose end people separate without addressing are leaving friends. Leaving people you've grown to care for and love without acknowledging that you are leaving, is in fact a loose end that deserves to be tied up. Most people have going away parties, and some people like to swiftly vanish with no trace of them ever having been there. But believe me, in this day and age of social media, you're gonna get the, "you seriously left without coming to say goodbye to us?" You may not realize it, but people do like you, whether it's that one Staff NCO who used to bust your balls every morning, or the lady at the sandwich shop who knows your order, your name, your kid's name, and your birthday. Make your rounds and say goodbye to people you've interacted with. It's a nice thing to do, and it is good practice for not burning bridges.

A huge loose end that people forget to tie up is leaving the service without paying your debts to people who have done you a solid. Don't be the guy who dips out on a debt you owe. This burns bridges, and remember what we talked about with those bridges. You don't want to leave on bad terms with anyone, or even leave any room for people to speak ill of you behind your back to others who may or may not be offering you employment later, or even a letter of recommendation for school or work. Leave on a high note, where people will respect the person you are, and not speak of you in disgrace.

Months and months up to even a year before you EAS—figure out if you're financially ready to separate. There are *thousands* of homeless veterans on the streets today. Hell, I was living on a friend's couch until I got my act together. Unless you're moving back home with the family, you are going to need a cash flow for the necessities. I get it, "where am I going to get money now, when I've only got a few months left?"

SAVE.

It's not easy, and I'd be lying if I told you I did the same thing, but I now know the benefit and envy those friends who weren't always spending money on the weekends, or on dumb things like the 200+ DVDs I accumulated in Okinawa. The earlier you start saving, the easier it is to separate from the service. Hell… you're the one EAS'ing! Instead of blowing all your money on a going away party/weekend… people should be treating *you* to drinks and dinner.

Unfortunately I *wasn't* ready. I had to pull out my Thrift Savings Plan, otherwise known as the TSP. Doing this cost me a 10% early cash out fee—on top of what the federal and state government wanted from my sudden increase in income. But I had to, in order to survive. By any means necessary, if you can manage without touching that retirement money you've been working for, do yourself that favor and wait it out. But if you absolutely need it, look into taking out a loan from your retirement fund, instead of cashing out. It'll cost you a lot less in the long run, and keep your retirement account working for you.

The last loose end you may have that I'll mention, are any legal matters hanging over your head. It is in your best benefit to ask *all* of the questions you may have before you EAS. Make legal send you away for being a nuisance, before you leave the military still in the dark about a situation you need clarification on. The branch of service you serve in most likely won't let you separate until all of your court issues are final, but if you have special situations going on for instance finding yourself in the middle of a divorce or a child custody hearing, and you don't fully understand how it plays out by you not having a job in a few weeks or months, ask. If you had been convicted in a court martial and had never served any time, and you want to know if you're going to be classified as a convicted felon when you separate… ask.

That last example is something I know very well.

I made the mistake of taking the word of my defense attorney and left the Marine Corps after being found guilty in a General Court Martial, being busted down two ranks, finishing my enlisted obligation, picking up Corporal before getting out, and still getting out honorably. After appealing my conviction twice and not getting the attention I felt like I should've had, I was told that my next step for *justice* was to talk to my Congresswoman. And that's just what I did.

I EAS'd and immediately went to my congresswoman's office, handed them a full court transcript with everything marked showing why I should've never been convicted, and asked, "what are my next moves, and options?" The congresswoman's office didn't know and the only thing I could be told is that, this matter was a military matter. The congresswoman has no jurisdiction over what happened in the Marine Corps. After that devastation I called back to the legal offices at my last duty station in order to get things squared away, and you know who else wasn't willing to answer my questions… that's right, my lawyer and everyone in that office, because "out-of-sight-out-of-mind."

There is going to come a day when you're no longer able to freely get what you need done on base, or be able to see the right person to get questions answered face-to-face. There is going to be a time where you won't get to have full access to records—freely, or have some of the benefits of being on the base, like getting free passports or free teeth cleanings! There is going to be a time where you may have wished simply to talk out a fight between you and a friend, or even repay a favor to someone very important to you.

Life is a lot faster out here in the civilian world, and definitely not as forgiving. If there are loose ends you have with anything or anybody… tie those loose ends up. Tie them up so you can EAS without feeling like you left something behind, or wishing you had done something that is now out of reach.

Remember: *You are separating from the service. Make sure you've taken care of yourself and your obligations, and make sure you leave feeling good about what you're about to leave behind.*

WHO ARE YOU? WHO AM I?

Once I separated from the Corps in February 2010, I took three months off for some much needed playtime. I hadn't taken leave to come see my friends and family for close to three years at that point, so I had made the decision that I was going to spend three solid months of time to myself in California with my people! After that three-month vacation I would then return to Okinawa to be with my then wife who was a schoolteacher on base, then further figure out a living plan.

The months from February to April were amazing. I'd partied hard, and gotten to spend some quality time with a lot of people I'd missed and rarely gotten to see. I'd gone to bars, and clubs, movies, beaches, amusement parks, and Vegas. I'd even gotten to go to weddings of my closest friends, and parties were thrown in my honor! It was seriously a great time.

But in the midst of all that, I was also going through personal confusion because my wife and I had been on the severe downfall of our marriage; my calls would go unanswered, and I could feel the hot knife slicing into the cold stick of butter when we did talk.

Around the same time, my best friend proposed to his wife and asked me to be his best man, and simultaneously my wife had told me to not come back home and asked for a divorce.

Shock and relief. Sadness and relief. A sense of knowing already that this had happened months and months before this day had surrounded me in a cocoon of confusion and liberation, and it was that day my life had changed. Party mode me had almost instantly disappeared, and the gung-ho, determined Marine had just been introduced to my friends.

I knew immediately that I needed shelter, a job, a car, and money. Late night rendezvous with my closest friends slowed down from nightly to weekly, and my focus on becoming employed was something that my friends had never seen from me. They all knew me as "Fun-Bobby" and not "Focused Bobby." So this shift of my professionalism, and dedication to improving my situation was taken differently than I had imagined.

After a while of me not being as available as I had been when I first got back into town, my friends—the closest people in my life, told me to my face that they didn't know me anymore. They said that I had changed. I was called out and hassled about the changes I had made and the new person I had become. Once I'd started working at my new company, mixed in with 60 and 70-hour workweeks, as well as spending my free time with my new girlfriend, things *had* changed.

My focus was different. That military mentality of mission first was on autopilot, and the ridicule from my friends made me care less about seeing them. I hadn't changed, they just stayed the same. I felt that they didn't understand what it was I was going through and I felt like by me being around, I was just filling a void with nothing substantial except being a fourth person in the car going for another night out on the town. For it seemed that every time I was with them, I felt I needed to be the court jester that I had been in our youth, and even though I can still be that guy, I didn't like feeling obligated to be that guy.

I couldn't understand why they couldn't see what it was I was doing and be happy for me.

It got so bad that one of my best friends called me and told me I had to meet him for dinner. A man notorious for dropping friends with no quarrels about it, sat me down and told me that if he didn't care about our friendship, I would've been in the history books. He told me that I had been missing out on some solid life drama that he was having, and that he missed *me*—and not just the funny guy that they were seemingly expecting to be around.

The fact is—my friends had a memory of me, as I had a memory of them. They were still closer to my memory than I was to theirs, meaning they remembered me much different than I had become, but not vice-versa. Life went on for all of us, but life is much different in the military. As servicemen and women, we may enlist as 17-year olds, but we come out in our early 60's. We may get into trouble still, and are hard-headed, heavy drinking, nit-picky, irrational-in-thought, rude, yet respectable and caring—but as veterans we *are* a different type of person. Believe it or not, we're a little more skeptical of people, and we don't take as much shit as we used to. We're more poised than we had been, and we know when to turn off the bullshit and get to work. We don't know how to talk to civilians anymore, and our levels of sympathy and empathy need some work.

It is important for us to reevaluate who we are and who we'd like to be on the outside world.

Things are different now. My friends all are married now and have kids, and they too are finding themselves going out less and less. They are changing and in-process of still changing their lives, and that laser focus I once had, I see it in them. There's no more hostility going on now, and we hardly see each other anymore, but it makes the get-togethers much more dynamic and more memorable when we do.

You're going to come back to a world that *once* knew who you were. They may still know who you are, but they will never fully understand a lot of what you're going through or what you're feeling. By no means is that grounds for breaking off friendships, it's just a sign that we still need some re-adjustment time, and some work on getting to know people once again.

Remember: *Life went on after boot camp, and having the expectation for the whole equation to be the same when you separate and come back home is a sure way to become dissatisfied or even depressed. You are a different person now than when you first joined the service. That's neither good nor bad. Just remember... you don't need to be the puzzle piece on somebody else's board to be a part of the big picture.*

How to Grow a Beard

It's Time for Lunch

I hadn't been at my new job for a whole three days yet, and the corporate world was incredibly different to me. I was in slacks and a different shirt every day, I didn't have to report to anyone in the morning (although I did for the first week until my supervisor told me to knock it off), and I was essentially on my own, expected to catch up on knowledge and pick up the slack on the project handed to me. So far, civilian life was cake.

All day, people would come by my cubical and ask who I was? Where I came from? What I'm working on? I would have answers for most questions, and be highly uncertain about others. I didn't know who I could trust and who was fishing for information that they could use against me. I was basically on a solo mission for acceptance from the right people.

This happened for the majority of the day, unless that part of the day was 11:30.

Around 11:30, the number of people stopping by my cube lessened—in fact, it came to a stop. The office got quieter. Foot traffic went away. And like a groundhog, I popped my head out of the cube to see where everyone was, and if they're lining up for lunch somewhere.

The first day my direct supervisor and the director took me out for lunch. I was given the "what we expect out of you" spiel, ate light, and when we got back to the plant I got back to work. That second and third day I couldn't find anyone in my group that I reported to during those lunch hours, so I didn't leave to eat lunch.

Day four, once the pitter patter of people's feet slowed down, and the office levels had gotten quieter, I popped my head up once again and asked my cubicle neighbor, "how's this lunch thing work out? Is there a bell, or does someone come around telling you its ok to go to lunch?"

You see for *years*, I had been conditioned to wait for the okay to go to lunch. I would never have fathomed going to lunch without the approval of a superior Marine telling me that I was okay to leave and be back in formation in front of squadron at 13:15. So in the civilian world my mindset was no different. So I waited for someone to come tell me I could go to lunch.

My cubicle neighbor told me that once it's lunchtime, we just go. Go eat and come back. Some of us only have about 30 minutes, but nobody is really keeping track as long as you put in your 8 hours. This was a new concept to me.

There was another situation where I had been asked to meet at "Joe's" desk at a specific time. I had no idea why I was asked to meet him at the time, so I showed up fifteen minutes prior, stood outside of his cubicle in a modified parade rest, and waited for him to show up, just to find out that: 1) he was the wrong Joe who requested my presence, 2) I looked stupid standing in front of his cubicle, let alone *anyone's* cubicle at modified parade rest, and 3) nobody wants you to show up fifteen minutes prior to an internal meeting, because this isn't the military anymore.

Again… new concepts to me!

There will be so many things you catch yourself doing that aren't normal as a civilian, which was normal for you while serving. I had to relearn something so insignificant as leaving to lunch on my own!

To this day I think it's hilarious.

Remember: *Working in the civilian world is new, and many companies are going to give you freedoms you'd longed-for for so long. Don't be afraid to ask about certain situations. A closed mouth, literally, never gets fed.*

How to Grow a Beard

"I've Never Been Treated Like This in my Life"

Those are actual words that were said to my supervisor, by a coworker at the company I had hired on with. However, in order for you to *really* understand why it was said, here's a little back-story...

JJDIDTIEBUCKLE. Marines will recognize this as an acronym that stands for: Judgment, Justice, Dependability, Integrity, Decisiveness, Tact, Initiative, Endurance, Bearing, Unselfishness, Courage, Knowledge, Loyalty, and Enthusiasm. If you never heard of this, I'm sorry and it's ok.

JJDIDTIEBUCKLE is an acronym that stands for our fourteen leadership traits, and these have been instilled in every Marine since the beginning of our service obligations. Some Marines hold these traits as word-is-bond, and some Marines excel at few and struggle at others. I feel like I embody these traits fairly well, and I don't like being tested about it. So when I was being treated like a child in my new role as a civilian employee and my project was being compromised by lazy, irrational, and unjust behavior—believe that I had something to say.

Okay, a little further back...

When I was hired on in my new role as a specialized field engineer, I was informed that it was my duty to know as much about the system mechanically and electronically as I could, as well as learn the general workings of other people's jobs. The reason being, was because my job required that I would have to be one of two people taking the systems that we were building out of the country to install them on the customer's sites. So naturally, I figured it would be wise to be extremely proficient and almost meticulous with my first system.

As months went by, by displaying hard work and a good hold of knowledge on the system I was working on, I was given the honor and trust by my supervisor to be named the team lead for the first few systems being sent off—starting with the one I had been working on for the last few months. This system was now *my* baby, and I was going to show the leadership who had put faith in me that their decision would ultimately be beneficial for all of us. That required me to be as capable here in this role, as I had been in the Corps.

You see, in the Marine Corps (and I'm sure all the other services), you get put into one of two categories; leaders or troops. The leaders didn't have to do all the slave driven jobs, and were basically given a task, with full expectation and trust that the jobs will get done proficiently and in a timely manner. The leaders may also have troops working directly under them. While the leaders made sure the jobs and tasks were being accomplished, there wasn't a lot of questioning, or back talk from anyone including higher leadership. Troops only pushed your buttons if you allowed it, but no matter how much your troops may have hated you or hated the situation you were in at the moment, the task at hand was *always* done proficiently and professionally.

The troops, however, were given small tasks to show that they could be trusted with larger tasks, or even tested with a job to see if they would finish or ask for help when they were stuck, instead of continuing to do things incorrectly. They hated the way they were treated, except the irony is, some of them were treated that way because they brought it upon themselves. Until they started picking up on what it took to be a leader, they stayed part of the troop.

Me—I was a leader. Nobody ever seriously questioned my direction. I was given basic instructions often and trusted to *make it happen.* If I'd succeeded, my team got all the credit. If something went wrong in the process, I took full responsibility and all the blame—never my crew. I *knew* when to take a step back and place my pride behind me.

But it's not like that in the civilian world. When you get out of the service and into a new job, people will do one of two things. They will feed you, or they will fear you. What I mean by that is that, people will be so happy that you, a veteran, are now working along side of them. You are a hero. You are selfless. You are charming, and funny, and a little mysterious.

Other people will size you up, and see you as a threat. You're a much quicker learner than they had been, you're wiling to work long hours to please your new boss, you don't complain about the same things they do, you're self-motivated and a hard worker, and a lot of people you come across are going to be simply intimidated by you even breathing the same air they do. And it was that guy, *the fearful*, who challenged me by undermining who I was and how I was raised for the last ten years before accepting this job.

You see, I had picked up on that project I was working on relatively quickly. I learned immediately that procedures and policies had to be followed strictly because we not only had to meet customer requirements, but we also had an internal Quality Control that held gold standards for the product we were building. So when a gentleman twice my age was interfering with forward progress because of an Alpha male standoff, I simply told him to "leave my project and get the fuck out of my face. Your integrity is shit and I don't need you around." This was in lieu of some loud finger snapping and maybe a knife-hand near the face.

The Quality Control inspector broke up what he thought was going to be a fight, and what I'd known as me simply giving a direct order to a lazy excuse-maker and nothing else. Lo and behold, I received a call from my supervisor, and I was asked to meet him and another factory manager in a conference room later that day. After hearing my version of what happened, and already having heard the other party's version, he simply says to me, "Graves, you're not in the Marine Corps anymore. You can't talk to people like that. You need to put a collar on that devil dog inside of you and shorten the leash."

Being that I was being told that by my Marine Corps veteran boss—I heard him loud and clear. Ever since that day, I have never been the same.

What had essentially confused me was that I believed I was hired because I knew how to get things done in a timely fashion—with no reason to be micromanaged, or told to do things twice. I figured that at this company, I would be able to do my job, with little-to-no internal resistance. The only people I had to worry about, ever, were those on the receiving side of the work—never those who were working with me. So getting the job done my way, the way I believed I was hired for, just wasn't going to work anymore.

I had to change my approach.

It is imperative. Civilians don't fully understand the veteran. We can get down on their level, but we can never expect them to work up to ours. In order to survive at this job I had to become a much more timid and a much more reserved individual, learning when to speak, and whom to speak with.

Demanding things, barking orders, or even lowering an octave to get your point across is threatening to a civilian in the work place, and you will be see as a hostile threat and that could very easily get you sent to HR, or even worse sent home—for good.

When I was told to put a leash on and stop being a Marine, it affected me. There was a fire that raged, and it had to be replaced by a flameless candle. It affected my goals in the company, it affected my work ethic, and my physical health. That had subconsciously made me feel that it was bad to be that person that I held up to the highest standard, and I felt that if that version of me were to show face again, I'd be reprimanded—again.

Regrettably my concerns *were* legit, because the minute I spoke up about some other things I felt were not right during a much later incident, people felt threatened and took me to HR.

How I got through my day-to-day in the workspace is that I became more soft-spoken. I started making sure people were comfortable with me by really getting to know people, and really putting myself out there. I knew people's birthdays and kid's names, and even their kid's birthdays. I kept track of the small stuff like checking in on someone if I knew they had a vacation or was going to the doctor's office. I stopped into my director's office just to say "hi" once in a blue moon. I wanted people to know that if anything ever happened like that again, that it must've been for a reason, because Robert is a *super* nice guy. So far, that has worked in my benefit.

What I saw as walking the walk by standing by my morals and judgments for a company whom I felt ultimately needed what I brought to the table, they saw as bullying and a creation of a hostile work environment. What I saw as me making sacrifices to make others comfortable working with me in order for job security, they saw me being a team player.

We as veterans are going to see things differently than our civilian counterparts or our coworkers. It's inevitable. Your fire inside to be *great,* will burn hotter than they could've ever imagined. The majority of you reading this will have a similar situation—guaranteed, and by no means am I saying to cower down and play nice. But understand this; how you bounce back and make yourself invaluable afterwards is what gives you your power back. You have to learn the new rules of the new game, and then master *that* game.

Remember: *You have to be flexible as you start to work with civilians. They're going to like a lot of what you bring to the table, but not everything. Don't walk into your new roles without humility. Know that you don't know it all. Understand that change, whether right or wrong, is inevitable. But be fluid, so you can form to any situation you are placed in.*

> "Empty your mind, be formless. Shapeless, like water. If you put water into a cup, it becomes the cup. You put water into a bottle and it becomes the bottle. You put it in a teapot it becomes the teapot. Now, water can flow or it can crash. Be water my friend."
>
> *-Bruce Lee*

FIND YOURSELF A MENTOR

Know that as you EAS and join the civilian sector, you are not re-inventing the wheel. You are not the first veteran to just get out of the military and start fresh, and you won't be the last. You aren't the first veteran to not have an idea what to do with your life, or what you should declare your major to be in college. And you won't be the first veteran who may not have saved up enough money to start on your own at all and have to take in a roommate or two just to make it.

Know that other people have been in your shoes.

So when I met a retired Master Gunnery Sergeant at my new company, I instantly knew I had someone to turn to when I needed someone to help me figure out this new life. In fact, I remember many different times I walked into his cubical when I first started and said, "this can't be what the civilian world is like."

Many times when I went to him, he reminded me of who I was and to not drop my pack around here. Many times he reminded me of how the people in this company don't care about you as a person, so be careful who you trust. And many times I wanted to tell him how crazy and overly cautious he was, but then I'd see the reality of what happens in big companies like the one we were in. Layoff after layoff... guys getting fired for hiring into the wrong job at the wrong time... backroom deals, and employees getting cut after giving the company 33-years, so the company can save money.

As much as I wanted to blow off his skepticism, he was right. He had been out here experiencing this world long enough that he sounded jaded. But in actuality, he was just...seasoned. He'd been in my shoes, in a situation similar to mine. My mentor was just passing on learned knowledge that he accumulated over the years.

WHAT CAN A MENTOR OFFER YOU? Someone you can call a mentor should have walked in your shoes before, or at least have the institutional intelligence to empathize or relate to similar situations of what you are or will be going through. A mentor may be in a position that you wish to hold one day in the future, or even someone you simply admire or look up to professionally.

A good mentor will always have a free ear to listen to you, and tough skin to know that your frustrations are not directed at them. A mentor can hear what you are saying without physically saying anything, and have the ability to stop you in your tracks and get you on the right path when you are seemingly in a state of confusion or in a standstill. But most importantly, a good mentor will pull you to the side and put a foot in your ass when you're in the wrong—holding you accountable for your actions.

Find a Mentor

My mentor was still a man with his own shit going on, and he was still in a role that being friends with coworkers could affect performance. This wasn't his first rodeo in the working world, and I'm sure it won't be his last. He and I had our own blow out in the job place, one that could only take place between Marines, and it broke our bond. Over time it pieced back together, but ultimately the Marine Corps will be our most solid bond, and I know forever I could walk up to him and rely on whatever it is I need from him and vice versa.

He often reminded me that we are not like them— the civilians who've never served. He often reminded me to not drop my pack. I respect him greatly, and even if he wouldn't call himself my mentor per se, he seriously was one of the first mentionable Marines I met on the outside, and I know that he had my best interest at heart. That Master Guns is a stubborn, old, selfish, inconsiderate, and petty dude, but he's also compassionate, caring, professional, and sincere, and I'm a better man because of him (not solely because of him... I wouldn't give you that much credit Greg).

Ask your mentor for tricks of the trade. Ask your mentor if they see areas for improvement, or even simply ask for feedback on your performance or direction in your personal and professional life. Make sure whomever you choose as a mentor has your best interest at heart and is on the same trajectory of where you might like to see yourself. A good mentor will want you to succeed as bad as you want to succeed.

Remember: *You are not alone out here. Remember, veterans will watch out for one another, but there will be some that will actually help you become a better person. Not because it benefits them, but because you deserve to have someone have your back, veteran or not! Find someone to pick their brains about what it's like to start fresh, how to acclimate to your new situations, and what it takes for people like us, veterans, to be successful in our new roles.*

A Lesson in Humility

Sorry to say, but your rank does not matter in the real world. When you get out you're as powerful as the job title you're given, and then realistically— you may be the new guy for a while. What does that mean? That means that all the professional respect you earned while in the service, you have to earn again. Nobody knows who you are, and all they know is that you served—which fortunately does go a long way.

However, respect isn't given. And civilians *are* skeptical of the new guy. I mentioned earlier on, that when you get out of the service and into a new job, people will do one of two things: they will feed into you, or the will fear you. Your new associates will test you. They'll want to find out if you're like them or if you are a threat. They don't know what you're capable of, and frankly you don't have the time nor the obligation to give them a tutorial.

In my new company that I hired on with, I'd had that finger-snapping, knife-handing, voice-elevating altercation earlier in the year, with that individual at my company who questioned my authority on my project. However, there have been other times, from other colleagues, that similar disrespect had been flagrantly thrown around.

I specifically remember being out of the country on a long job and running a performance test in front of my customers, when we ran into a software snag that had been overlooked. At this point I had been a part of the company for close to 2 years, and had already proved my worth by showing that I was able to hold my own and be the face of the company in place of managerial positions. The customer wanted to talk to one of the developers of the system I was selling off, and so we called *the* developer.

This guy had a really bad reputation at the company for being lazy, irresponsible, and a little bit of a fibber. For sure, he was the epitome of a *Blue Falcon, Brovo Foxtrot, Buddy Fucker...* or whatever your preferred term is. As I sat there on speakerphone with him from the outskirts in the middle of nowhere, working on my Thanksgiving, he says in front of God and everyone, "I don't know why you're even on that program. They should have sent someone more experienced and more qualified."

Now I had learned from earlier altercations that the way to success was having *emotional intelligence*, so this was something that we had to settle sometime later, sometime after the fire that I had initially called to put out in the first place. He was extremely out of line, and needless to say it never happened again. But these are the things that go on.

There isn't a sense of the same military camaraderie out here with civilians, and unfortunately the same can be true when you have multiple veterans working together.

A great friend of mine was one of those guys who told the same stories as many times as you'd let him tell it. But he was a fantastic storyteller, so you really never interrupted, and just listened to the stories again and again. He told me a story about this Marine he had worked with way back in the day, and as a civilian—this Marine used to seriously pull rank on him. This guy got out as an old Gunnery Sergeant and came into to the new job with a puffed out chest, in super Alpha-male mode.

My friend, an old Air Force guy, and this Gunny at one point were really tight in the beginning. But then the Gunny started showing his Devil Dog side, and instead of listening to direction in his new company, he "wanted to run the show" (my friend's words, not mine). Now I know the mentality of both services. One service is more easy going than the other, and the other is pretty neurotic… for the best intentions though. And when this old Gunny came into my friend's work territory barking orders and demanding respect as the new guy, well let's just say there was a conflict of interest.

Fists almost starting flying.

The problem was that the new Marine/employee/veteran wasn't playing by the rules. When we get hired on as a new employee, we are hired on because we are *capable* of doing the job we were hired on to do, **but** we still have learning to do.

Unless you're hired back onto base as a liaison, more often than not you're going to have to learn new protocols, follow new directions, and change perspective on what it is your role is in the job. The hats you wear may change, where once you may have been a troop leader, and now you're just a troop.

Change is good. Change is fine. But humility is key. Understand that you don't and won't know everything, so be humble enough to reach out for help and ask questions. Be humble enough to listen, and leave your ego at the door. You didn't know how to run a shop when you were an E-3—no, you had to move up in the ranks and office structure... the same applies out here.

In due time...

Remember: *Rank doesn't carry over. It will help you to not start at the very bottom, but you have to prove you deserve the respect again. You don't have to stop working with the dedication and mindset you had while you were in, but when it comes to working with other people... other vets in particular, it's better to start off with the mutual respect that you are both qualified and have* *been hired on for a reason. But you have some learning to do again before you can be the boss.*

How to Grow a Beard

Leave Your Potty Mouths in the Shitter

I remember a little after I first enlisted, hazing started to become an extremely hot topic throughout the Marine Corps. We couldn't make fun of *anyone*, much less lay our hands on someone or have hands laid upon us. I remember joining a Marine Corps where my first drill instructor, Sgt. Beltran, picked me up by my neck and put me onto the top bunk... and as crazy as it sounds, I respected him more for that. I knew what I was getting into when I enlisted, and although I'm not sure if the punishment fit the crime, it happened, and it adds to my Marine Corps story.

I visited the MCRD recruit depot a little over a year later, and I'm guessing he put his hands on the wrong recruit because he called my name from out of the shadows, and as I locked up at attention, he told me to relax and invited me over to just come shoot the shit with him like a man. He told me how he was being closely watched because of laying his hands on a recruit recently, and told me that his job and rank were on the line. He wished me well, and I'd never heard from him again. Last I heard, rumor had it he'd been busted down to Lance Corporal... but that could be a rumor.

The point of that story was that in a blink of the eye, a man, a machine, a warrior—went from America's hero to America's savage, and the same can easily be just as similar in the civilian world. The times of coming into work and finding somebody to pick a fight with in the office, a.k.a. the arena of gladiators, are no more. The times of walking in and throwing around vulgarities, racial and ethnical slanders, homophobic remarks, religious shots, screaming about ripping peoples balls off, or how many hookers you were in on deployment… leave that shit in the service. Even though the military is like being a part of an extended family, it is also a place of employment. You can get away with a lot more foolery in the service than you can outside of it, but many of you know, that too is slowly changing.

Once there was a Marine we knew whose girlfriend took a picture of him wearing her clothes. She sent it via text to a few people in his shop and then it spread like wild fire around the unit. So fast that we had a company formation on hazing this specific individual, and if you were caught even looking at him funny, you'd find yourself facing NJP.

What we once saw as tough love and as "boys being boys" in the service, the civilian side sees inappropriate conduct and offensive behavior… and there is absolutely no place for it out here in the civilian world or in the work force. The civilian world is very Politically Correct, and take it from me, you will turn a lot of heads and rub people the wrong way if you maintain the same exact personality you had while you were serving in the military.

I can't speak for everyone when I say those days are done. I'm not saying that all of us acted like that in the service, and sure, there will be some jobs where you can still act like you're in a fraternity. But what I can do is tell you this as clear as I can—in the professional working world, there is no room for us to act like we're still shooting the shit with our buddies in the barracks. People frown upon it, and are extremely eager to get you out of their safe bubble. People really do take people to HR; it's not just something you see on TV.

Get in tune with your softer civilian side, and embrace the fact that you had that second life—full of dick jokes and long unnecessary drinking nights that led to God knows what type of shaming that only your military family will find amusing. There will be moments when you get around some servicemen and you can share those stories once again, or maybe even share some of those stories with close civilian friends or close coworkers. However, when it comes to large public forums or the workplace, just remember there is a place, and a time—and it's most likely not in front of your civilian employers.

Remember: *There is a place and a time for you to re-live the "good ol' days." Know your audience. Know the crowd. And just ask yourself, especially when you're at work, would my CO approve of this right now?*

How to Grow a Beard

CALL THE PROS

Once we finally separate from the service, life changes instantly. For one, we aren't the people we were when we left our homes, no matter how desperate you are to still be that person. The stories we have to share are like college dorm stories on steroids, and believe it or not you are a lot more mature now than you would have been had you not enlisted at all. Additionally, most of us learned some type of skill while serving in the military that we've done day in and day out, that makes you instantly marketable when you EAS and are ready to enter the civilian working world.

With our long laundry list of pro's and con's on the differences between being in the military and being a veteran, one huge mistake we make when we get out of the service, is that we are ridiculously gullible. We tend to listen to old salty vets who didn't really research anything on their own, and have created their own realities. We buy into the Negative Nancy's who didn't get a certain medical rating from the VA, and now are quick to curse the VA and everyone who works for or with the VA to the high heavens. We unquestionably believe our cousins who didn't finish college because they weren't exactly up to date on how the GI Bill worked. I see it time and time again from older veterans who lost their GI Bill benefits or didn't utilize their VA loan in order to purchase a home.

It is sincerely upsetting. For you to have served your country, and not be informed properly of what you rate and what you don't... that's a crime. (*Now it's clearly not a crime literally, and if you believed that, you may want to really pay attention to the message in this chapter*).

Almost always, TAMP/TAP will give you a list of your rights and benefits before you get out. But before you get out, do yourself a favor and run a search on what exactly you rate in your state, or even as a general veteran citizen of the good ol' U S of A. There are pell grants for veterans and their spouses, there are home loans and special refinance rates available specifically for you. There are special business loans and programs created solely for veteran entrepreneurs. It doesn't sound like much, but when you greatly reduce your competition by over 90% of the US population (since veterans only make up somewhere up to 6% of the US population), and assuming even less of a number of veterans are applying for the same programs you are, or even at all... if you qualify and you seek out the assistance, I say the odds are in your favor.

WHAT I LEARNED ABOUT STARTING A BUSINESS. If you are still in the service and are about to separate, and you think you may want to start your own business at some point when you get out, I urge you to ask your TAMP/TAP coordinator to get you familiar with the BOOTS TO BUSINESS transition group. They would be able to extensively walk you through the process of becoming the entrepreneur you've dreamed of always being.

I did not do this. I learned slowly how to run a business, how to market myself, how to spend money, all by making mistake, after mistake, after mistake.

Starting a business is hard work, but it's the most rewarding thing you can do, especially after working for someone else for so long. It creates some *Esprit de Me*—some feeling of pride in yourself that only you can have for your accomplishments, or even the fact that you put yourself out there and tried to set yourself apart from the others.

Spend your money wisely on marketing tools. Really think three or four times about your approach. I worked for a Master Gunnery Sergeant who would say "Remember the 6-P's Marines: *Proper Planning Prevents Piss Poor Performance.*" It comes to mind now, but as a man who so desperately just wanted to branch off from the corporation I had worked with for so long—I wildly and ignorantly threw money into advertisement stationary (such as cards and pamphlets), without having second eyes on my verbiage or spelling. I also never even asked someone who had already succeeded in the market I was moving into, if what I was doing was worth the effort of reaching the masses.

Something I also learned is that you will be the only person you can rely on at first. You will have a drive and a focus that others won't understand. You will believe in your product more than anyone else, and that means it's on you, and you alone to really get it moving. People will say they're in your corner often, and one of the biggest things I've learned is that as a veteran with a plan—as a person who has drive and a fire in your eyes, you will attract people who want to ride your wave. They want in on what it is you're bringing to the table, and they will sell themselves to you as a friend, a comrade, and a business partner you can trust. Being that you want to grow so big, so bad, this is where we become gullible.

Be very cautious of whom you let around you, and who you let into your business plans. You may find yourself off track very easily, or even doing double the work, while still holding onto a belief that you and whomever it is you have put trust into, are still going to work on *your* dream. It's almost like when you win the lotto. People will come out the woodwork to be your friend and family once again, just to pitch their ideas about how your money should be spent.

Don't get me wrong! It's not necessary to write everyone off as soon as they make mention of business related issues.

Listen with an open mind, talk about what it is they are bringing to the table. Write out a timeline and a business plan, some goals for both you and the individual, and then monitor that plan often. Since you most likely will be a startup business, if that other person is not a paid employee of yours and wants to be a partner, then you shouldn't have to micromanage them—they should be on the same motivational level you are, and share the same intentions.

Lastly, if the relationship isn't working out, or if your ideas are not taking form and you feel like you're being held back... cut the ties. You've got work to do, and you can't afford to have anyone holding you back.

What I learned about going to school. If you take anything from this book, understand this. If you don't use it, you lose it. SO MANY PEOPLE that I know who served did not utilize their educational benefits. And the majority of them regret it. I haven't met one person who hadn't utilized the benefits and have said to me, "good thing I didn't get my education when it was free to me."

Whether you are ready right out of the military or not, as it stands today you have ten years to use the Montgomery G.I. Bill and fifteen years to use the Post 9/11 G.I. Bill. That's a long time to sit on free money and free education, and then let it go to waste.

Even though I had sat through all those educational briefings and college counseling sessions, I found out that I was still unaware on how to maximize what I was getting out of the educational benefits. You see, I started working toward my Psychology degree while I was serving in Okinawa in 2003, when I first got back from Afghanistan. I finally finished my Associate Degree and I started on my Bachelor in 2009. When I separated in 2010, I had been hired by a company who could care less about my education, but more about my hands-on experience. So education took a back seat to my life plans.

In 2012 I figured I'd take a course or two at a time, and opted to use my Chapter 30, otherwise known as the Montgomery G.I. Bill. Even knowing that I was going to finish my major in Psychology, someone (another misinformed veteran) had gotten into my head and told me it was a bad idea to change from one benefit to the other because the educational benefits don't always transfer over. So I was talked into believing that I shouldn't use my Chapter 33 (Post 9/11 G.I. Bill) because I was almost done with this degree and I should just wait for Grad school.

Listening to that awesome advice lost me a potential $10,000+ in housing allowance, which I could've had in my pocket to help pay the bills and make life a little easier while I was going to school. You see, how *I* understood it was, that you don't get a housing allowance on the Chapter 30 benefits, but you have the freedom to use that benefit for specific trade schools and certifications; whereas the Chapter 33 benefits are for a degree specific plan and once you option to use the Chapter 33 benefits you can't option back to the Chapter 30. So basically, you are eligible for both initially, then when you choose to use the Post 9/11 G.I. Bill, you are no longer eligible for both. But don't let that sway you from using it.

Remember, I had to learn that lesson the hard way.

I've come to learn that there are very few things that the average college student *cannot* do with the Post 9/11 Bill. Even after I've received my Bachelor in Psychology, I enrolled into an accredited trade school for Hypnotherapy, and they were more than happy to work with the Chapter 33 benefits. I've contacted other schools for coaching, or other types of counseling programs, and even they are able to use the Post 9/11 for at least half of their schooling. I personally know others who've used their Post 9/11 for trade schools or other certification courses. You may not get the full housing allowance, but you will get some assistance.

Here's the secret benefit not many people I've talked to are aware of. Vocational Rehabilitation and Employment (Chapter 31). Understand that, the last thing that the government wants is for there to be a ton of unemployed and homeless vets (even though there are), so they created this program to help people get back on their feet and learn a new trade—or help them advance in their current trades by paying for school or certifications. Now, this is on a case-by-case basis, but I do know that if you will not finish your degree before your benefits run out, you are able to enroll in the Voc Rehab program and have at least an extra year of help. The key is to do this well before your education benefits run out, so you can continue to benefit from the housing allowance.

The last little known fact is that as it stands today you are able to get a Montgomery G.I. Bill refund. This pertains to people who bought into the Montgomery G.I. Bill. The qualifications are that you must have bought into it, you must be enrolled in the Post 9/11 G.I. Bill, used all your 36-months of the Post 9/11, you are the original beneficiary (meaning you didn't pass on the benefits to a family member), *and* you are receiving housing benefits that same month you run out of benefits. If you meet all those requirements, you'll get the $1200 you put into the Montgomery G.I. Bill.

Regardless of if you meet these requirements or not to receive the refund, there is no need to be out of the military and not utilize these benefits. You earned them, and even if you look at it as a way to make extra money in the beginning, you will benefit in the end. Whatever you do, don't take just anyone's word for what it is. ASK QUESTIONS. I can't tell you how many phone calls and cumulative hours I've been in the Student Center for Veterans. Every college has one. Find it. Use it. They will help you, and if they don't know an answer to your question, hold them to the fire to help you find it.

WHAT I LEARNED ABOUT BUYING A HOUSE. Depending on where you end up after the service makes a huge difference in whether you buy a house or not. I remember sitting in my shop in Okinawa, and a friend of mine was looking at a home in Texas. I asked him how much he was looking to pay and he said, "nothing more than $125,000." I laughed and told him he's not going to get anything for $125K. Then he laughed and showed me what he was looking at.

He was looking at a 4 bedroom/ 3.5 bath with an acre of land right outside of a big city in Texas. I was astonished. I told him to put those same requirements into the search, but search in Los Angeles. Then he was astonished to see that the cheapest place like that started at a mid $600K. For shits 'n giggles he put in that price in Texas, and basically could buy his own ranch mansion.

Being in the military for so long, and never really having known anyone who owned their own home, I didn't know a lot about home ownership. In fact, I wasn't even aware I could own my own place, because in my mind you had to be making at least $150,000 a year. Not until my friend found out that my wife and I were paying $1700 in rent in Los Angeles. He basically told me that I was practically paying his mortgage—and that's the exact moment I started to become serious about buying a home.

What we constantly hear from the civilians around us is that, "it's impossible to buy... It's a sellers market... You've got to have at least 10% of the down payment since the housing market had taken a hit." That was discouraging to hear. I'd figured I'd never get out of living in an apartment.

But then I started doing my own research. In fact, Navy Federal was very helpful in helping me find a realtor, and a home.

Unfortunately, if you use the VA loan, you can't have *any* home you want. When you find a house, you'll have to pay for inspectors, and the VA will also send their own inspector. The reason being is that they don't want the veteran to be on the shit end of the deal. As I've said before, people will take advantage of you, because the majority of us are not aware common real estate practices. Some sellers won't even accept the VA loan because of the hassle, so because of this, the house hunting process may go a little slower than how you'd like it to go.

Groups such as Navy Fed and USAA will help you from day one. Once you call them and say you're interested in buying a home, they will set you up with a realtor that they trust. These realtors are supposed to be fully knowledgeable on the ins and outs of the VA loans, but I assure you all of them are not. In fact, my wife and I called Navy Fed three separate times to request a new realtor before landing on the one who worked best for us.

Buying a home to live in is an important moment of your life, take the situation by the reigns and if you're not satisfied with the quality of work your realtor is doing for you, speak up. Ask questions. I promise you, a good realtor can change the game and make the house hunting process enjoyable and uncomplicated.

One last thing about buying a house, please, and I beg you... please plan accordingly. Know your financial situation before you go into this huge purchase. Really take a look at the "if" situations, such as, *"if I get laid off,"* or *"if we get a divorce"* will I be able to maintain a house payment, let alone the water, power, gas, cable, automobile, insurance, etc.? Only purchase a home if you know you're capable of being a homeowner. I learned the hard way.

We'd purchased in 2012 when the interest rates were at an all time low. Score! My wife had to move in without me because I was away on business travel for a while, and when I came back, I came home to a perfectly manicured green lawn, and a nicely cooled home. I had come back to step foot in my first home for the first time. Some weeks passed by and we received our first electric bill from Los Angeles Department of Water and Power, and I opened a $750 water and power bill.

Look—I'm a grown man, but I have no shame in saying I locked myself in the bathroom and cried.

I was shocked, traumatized, baffled, stunned, and whatever other adjective you think could possibly fit that scenario, all at once. I looked at that bill and immediately thought, "there's no way I can keep this up if this is how it's going to be. I see now why people default on their loans and go bankrupt." It turns out there was way more to being a homeowner than just paying mortgage and your cable bill.

Some months later I got a bill from the tax office asking me to pay the difference in property tax that the last owners hadn't paid. I did my research and it turned out that wasn't a scam and I actually had to pay that too. Then almost immediately we were having plumbing issues, and electrical issues. It was a monetary disaster.

Fortunately, we were able to gain some type of control on the water and power, even though during the summer months my bill can easily get up to $500 if we're not careful. But with upgrades, and paint, new energy efficient appliances, new furniture to fill the empty rooms, insurance, unexpected repairs, etc... these are the things nobody really tells you that you're going to be spending money on when you first buy your home. I had to sell stocks and run up credit cards to survive that first year. I would do it all over again if I had to in order to have this place my family calls home, *but* I wish someone would've given me the heads-up so I could've planned more appropriately.

This chapter has a lot of information that I learned from personal experience. I really just want you to pull from it that you can't go off of one person's experience (including mine), and it is imperative for you to do your own research and ask questions about your specific situations. Even though I'm writing all this from personal experience, it's just a template. I strongly advise you to make sure that what I said is still valid, so you are not walking blindly on someone else's word.

I've always had a saying that as humans we're like ants, and tend to follow the leader. If other veterans don't know and will lead you into the wrong direction, believe that civilians will do they same. Lastly, pass on the knowledge you receive to others looking for help—but make sure you're passing on accurate information and give them the source of the information, whether it be a phone number, a website or an email so they can research it themselves.

Remember: Everyone seemingly has your best interest at heart, but you really are the only one who has your best interest at heart. Do yourself a favor and diligently research anything anyone tells you. It's better to waste an hour on the phone on hold in order to talk to someone knowledgeable, than it is to start a process only to find out you are not eligible, have been doing something incorrectly, or could have been getting assistance all this time but haven't. Now is the time to use those small groups for vets.

SACRIFICE

What have we sacrificed to be where we are today? Oh so many things. A lot of us left friends behind. Great jobs. High school lovers. We may have left our dogs or our cars behind. Some of us have married, divorced, and remarried. Some people have lost families, and children. We've sacrificed our ability to say "I quit," and we've sacrificed our free time. We've sacrificed our bodies, and our lives for the greater population of the United States of America, and most importantly we've sacrificed our attention to the people who need it the most.

Sacrifice isn't a word we use a lot in the military because it's too common. Many have missed their children's births, or lost friends and relatives. Others have missed funerals, canceled weddings, or served duty holidays like Thanksgiving and Christmas. We have war heroes who've died or lost limbs, or worse... their minds. If you tell someone what you've sacrificed to be in the military it may fall on deaf ears, because sacrifice is the name of the game when you serve. We're used to it. It's common, like Monday follows Sunday. It's basically in our job description.

When you separate from the service, sacrifice may or may not be on a smaller scale, but understand—it's still sacrifice. You don't have to downplay what you're going through because you've been in, "worse situations."

For instance, my first job took me out of the country for 6+ months throughout the year. When I was out of the country, I got paid very well. When I was back home, I coined the term "*cube cash*," for the small amount of money I was making in comparison to being on the road. Being that I was stationed in Okinawa for five years during my enlistment, and went on multiple deployments and exercises, personally I was used to being on the road and away from family.

My wife and I would get into arguments all the time because of my "cold-heartedness" to being gone. I was conditioned for it, the feeling of "missing" someone was callused and affected me less than others. Often I told her that this was my job—so she'd have to suck it up, and then I'd throw the fact that I needed to be on the road to make the money that was paying for our lifestyle. But over the years I could see that the money wasn't important to her. Shit, after five years on and off the road, and seeing how poorly individuals were being treated in the company, the money wasn't important to me either.

I started *longing* to be home. My closest friends were hurt that I wasn't spending time with them. My wife was depressed and lonely—I started to understand the feeling of "missing" someone, and understand the feeling of being left out. I started to realize that my company loves hiring vets, because we were accustomed to being alone. But I didn't want to be alone anymore.

The months of staying in a hotel room and staying up until 2:00 am to Skype with the family were getting old. Being by myself in non-English speaking countries was getting old. Missing my friends' kids, my nieces and nephews grow up—that was getting old. Hearing the sadness in my wife's voice from me not being home for Thanksgivings, weddings, funerals... that was getting old.

The lie I told myself and my wife, that this is my obligation and this is how it has to be, became clearer. The more I was shitted on, I realized that I'm *not* in the Marine Corps anymore and I'm not obligated to this life. I may have not been advanced to the front lines at the time, or even wearing a uniform, but the fact I wasn't home, was a huge sacrifice that took a toll on my marriage.

I started looking around the company I worked at. Guys in my position who'd been there 20-30 years, were now all divorced twice, paying alimony and child support out of the ass. A lot of them were alcoholics, chain smokers, and they looked beat up; like if life dealt them one more bad hand they'd be one glass of whiskey away from turning the pistol on themselves. The more I saw them, the more I couldn't see myself in their position any longer.

Which is ultimately one of the bigger drives that pushed me to go back to school.

School was no different. Being a full-time student, and a full time employee required a lot of sacrifice too. Although I was home everyday, I wasn't available. I would leave to work around 6:30 am, and then leave from work straight to school—until 10:00 pm. If I wasn't at school, I was at work or writing a paper. Whatever it was, I was never home. By this point we'd had my son, and my wife started feeling what it was like to be a single mother.

Once again, I made the argument, that this has to happen—this is the only way I can stay home and be a father at some point down the line. Once again, she understood, but it doesn't take away the fact that I'm not home and I'm sacrificing my family life for something else—no matter what it is.

Sacrifice is the act of giving up something pleasurable, wanted, enjoyed, important to you, or simply just... special, for a different type of important act or item. Some people sacrifice smoking or drinking for their health, while others sacrifice love for money. However the fact remains that any type of sacrifice... **all** sacrifice, requires you leaving something behind that is a big part of who you are, for a separate reason. The worst part about sacrifice is that we all view it differently.

Take for instance a man who was raised in poverty where money was scarce in the home. The only way to survive was to work three jobs to make sure his family was provided for. He may feel that the need to sacrifice quality family time in order to make sure the bills were paid, and that the family lives above the lifestyle he grew up in is absolutely necessary. In fact he does not see that what he is doing is sacrifice at all, but instead the only way to survive.

Whereas the other side of that equation, if we take his wife who comes from a family-first lifestyle—a lifestyle that never had to worry about money, his wife may see leaving the family as the worst thing possible and would rather sacrifice material items in order to have quality time with her family.

Both individuals view sacrifice as losing one thing to gain another, but their values are different. Both can be rationalized, but ultimately it is unfair to ask someone to justify their sacrifice because your values have been established long before you consciously were aware of them.

So what I want to really concentrate on communicating is that however you *view* sacrifice... sacrifice *is* sacrifice, whether you're deployed in Iraq for a third time, sent out of state or country for your civilian job, or a full-time student. I like to tell the people I'm working with that, "***Your* problems *are* the biggest problems and just as important as**

anyone else's, because they're *yours*, and *you* have to deal with them… no one else."

Sacrifice affects you and those around you. Do not downplay the sacrifice you make today as a civilian, simply because while you were serving you deployed four different times and missed two of the four births of your children.

Any time that we take away from ourselves, our friends and our loved ones, it affects our psyche and our relationships to those people. And it's not fair to you, to hold yourself to a higher standard of what you constitute sacrifice to be, just because now you're a civilian. When it comes to sacrifice, just know that there is no level of standard set from your *past* life that should affect your current life and future.

Remember: *Don't sacrifice something you're not willing to lose while you're a civilian. Remember what's important to you and remember that you have options that will create compromise in your life.*

DO SOMETHING FOR YOU

My first tour in Okinawa, I was a stuck in the barracks. No fault of anyone but my own. I wasn't necessarily stuck there because I absolutely wanted to be in the barracks, but I was stationed there when dial-up was just getting to the barracks, and I'm sure cable wasn't available yet, so I wasted my money on things like buying DVDs from the PX. I don't even remember being able to watch AFN in the barracks at that time... so cut me some slack on the DVDs.

My friends loved to go out to clubs, and I was the bar guy myself... however, I was under-ranked and under-aged, and had to be back on base by 0000 with my libo buddy regardless of where we went. Going out turned into more of a hassle sometimes, especially since we weren't allowed to own cars in my unit until we were a NCO or married. Needless to say, the few things I got to really experience around the island came few and far between during my first tour—and I am completely aware that I am the only one at fault.

My second tour to Okinawa, I was married, and had picked up Sergeant. So I lived off base, and I had my own car. Life on the island was much more enjoyable. I found hobbies to get into, and explored the island more. I started getting into more activities and really started doing things for me—which in turn made life much more enjoyable and less stressful.

How to Grow a Beard

A good friend of mine was a diver and had talked my wife into getting me certified for my birthday. That certification course was one of the greatest things—to date—that I've ever gone through, because it's given me something that I can enjoy anywhere. My friend and I absolutely took advantage of the great diving in Okinawa. We would get our tanks filled at lunch, then go catch two dives after work. On the weekends, we'd wake up and get in the water by 9 am, and get home 12 hours later. I'd seen a universe that we weren't supposed to see, and interacted with a part of something completely different than my everyday life. Besides sports, diving had become my outlet.

When I first separated from the Marine Corps and came back to California, I decided I wanted to dive the kelp forest and possibly see seals or sharks, and so I signed up for a boat dive to Catalina. This would be my first time diving in California, and my first boat dive, not to mention my first dive without anyone I knew diving with me. Now understand I'm not the stereotypical diver you see in National Geographic magazines; I'm well over six feet tall, well over 250 lbs., and I'm half black, and I believe at that time I was trying to grow the largest ugliest beard I could possibly grow (protesting 10 years of shaving), so it wasn't a surprise that nobody took me seriously on that dive boat. Since I didn't sign-up with a friend, they stuck me with the goofiest, sloppiest dive buddy I'd ever seen in the ocean. It was almost a wasted trip for me, until at the end of the day one of the crew asked if I wanted to go down with him for the last dive. Unknowingly, he was checking me out for skill level, and when we came up, he recommended that I volunteer at the California Science Center.

So I looked into it.

I ended up with the opportunity to volunteer at the Science Center in their dive program, helping feed the marine life and taking care of the kelp tank, and I met some absolutely incredible people through it. Being a part of that program allowed me to hold on to a small piece of a larger piece of me that I knew in the Marine Corps. I didn't just get thrown out without an outlet. Being a part of the dive program at the Science Center gave me something to look forward to other than the grind of constantly looking for employment. It helped me to easily transition into being a civilian by moving from my military team, to a different type of team, and in-turn learning how to really communicate with non-military members.

Finding something to do out in the civilian world, for me, gave me a confidence that everything is going to be okay. It unconsciously assured me that transition into this world is possible. It allowed me to make new bonds almost instantly, and also created resources for references for job referrals.

Every veteran that I know that is doing well, found a group of people with their similar interest, and it has made transition easy for them. Whether it'd be playing Magic the Gathering, or hanging out at the tattoo shop. Cross fit, or Cross Stitch—if you find something for you outside of the service, more than likely, it will be much easier to transition from the military world.

I was lucky enough to accidentally find a diving group I enjoyed being around, however if you're not knowledgeable on finding groups that share similar interests, look on websites like *Eventbrite* or *MeetUp*. There's a *MeetUp* group close to every major city I've been to, as well as in different countries. If you're not familiar about the concept of these groups, these are essentially websites that brings groups of people with similar interests together by inviting each other to open invitational activities. So if you like sports, tap dancing, cooking, or even if you're trying to find a new church, there's usually something in your area, and all it takes is a small online search.

It's easy to spiral downward, and become depressed while your fresh out of the service. People will want to party with you for a few weeks, before the nostalgia has worn off. Then as they get back to their regularly scheduled lives... you should too. There's no reason to be *lost* in the civilian world when you get out. It's easier now, more than ever, to find like-minded individuals to surround yourself with, to help you transition back into the civilian world. Hell, you might even meet some veterans in the group that you can relate to, and could possibly help you get back on your feet.

Remember: *You need to find something for you. Something that is <u>your</u> outlet. Something <u>you</u> enjoy doing, so that <u>you</u> can have an outlet while in transition, or for as long as it benefits you. I promise you—you will need an outlet.*

How to Grow a Beard

GET FIXED!

While I was in the Marine Corps, I had four surgeries; two ankle, and two knee. Recently, I had my labrum repaired, and I give full thanks to the VA. Unfortunately, what had happened is, as a civilian I had become heavy and round. I decided one day I was going to get my life back and get back in shape, and that very same day I reinjured my shoulder. This was an 11-year-old injury, but as a young, dumb, and seemingly invincible, blood thirsty, hard core Devil Dog—I sucked it up, and lived on with it the whole time while I was serving in the Marine Corps.

Often I heard my dad's voice in my head when I got hurt in the Corps, *"Get up and rub some dirt in it."* I followed that to a "**T**." Still to this day if I'm out hiking or anywhere remote from civilization where some rubbing alcohol, peroxide, or some Neosporin is not available, I'll grab a handful of dirt and rub it into my cuts and scrapes. It was a way of how I could show I was hardcore, and that I absolutely belonged in the elite club of men and women that we call *the Few, the Proud.* In fact going to medical was frowned upon while you were young in the service. Often if you felt like death, we made the jokes to just take Motrin and water, and everything will be okay.

Then we'd actually go to medical—and they'd prescribe us Motrin and water.

If you had a light duty chit, especially before a hump or a physical fitness test, you were the center of all jokes, and often accused of being a malingerer, a broke dick, a faker, weak, scared, or any other adjective that would describe anything other than a warrior or a hero. To others, they might see you as the next Einstein, wondering why they didn't think of going to get a light duty chit.

Often, to show how extremely die-hard we were, we would push through PFT's with sicknesses like bronchitis, or go on a 10 mile hump with a strained calf, bad back, or a busted ankle. It built character. It gave us bragging rights. It showed "mind over matter"—*If you don't mind, it don't matter.* By no means am I saying that this is a bad thing, because it separated the categories of people you knew were going to give 110%, from the people who just wanted to be a part of the crowd. But I will say, if you don't get professionally medically checked out... it *will* catch up to you down the road.

Normally when I had downtime, I would get checked out. That's essentially how I had to have so many surgeries. But some never got checked on until *after* I got out of the service—and that's what I want to preach about today!

Healthcare

Once you get out of the service, you no longer have anything to prove to anybody. You've been pounding ground for so long in your boots, breaking the body down slowly *and* surely, that it's time for your body to get a tune-up. When you get out, make sure you register with the closest VA hospital near you.

Understand this: registering with the VA, and registering with the **VA hospital** are completely different, so much so, that they don't even share basic information records. There are three portions to the VA: The VBA (Benefits), and the VHA (Healthcare), and the National Cemetery. So make sure you register with the correct offices.

Once you register with the VA hospital, they'll set you up with an appointment to meet your primary care doctor. Be extremely honest, and if anything is wrong, get it checked. Be persistent in fixing *your* body.

When I first went in for my shoulder, they told me nothing was wrong—that my shoulder was just sore from prior activity, and to "ice it, and do these stretches on this paper I'm giving you to take home." Months went by and I went in again for the same issue. X-rays were taken… nothing wrong. MRI taken… nothing wrong. But I still felt the pain when I moved my arm and I insisted they find out what it was. They then injected dye into my shoulder and ran another MRI, and it was then they saw it—my torn Labrum inside my shoulder.

It took a while to find the issue, but because I was persistent and not taking "no" for an answer, I ended up having some of the best doctors from UCLA work on me. To me, it was a necessary fix if I were going to be a fully functional father and an active person again.

It's important to take care of yourself, because the short time you served, whether it'd be 4 years or 30, is just a scratch in time in relation to the age you can possibly reach in your lifeline. Not to mention the physical beatings you put on your body while serving in the military is *abnormal* compared to average civilians, and know this... "wear & tear" is real my friend.

Fortunately for me, being a combat veteran (which essentially is any military member who deployed in support of OEF/OIF/OND), the medical services were free for the first 5 years after I separated for any injuries categorized as *presumptive service connected*. That means the medical care was free, the medication was free, the hospital stay was free, and the follow up appointments, the physical therapy, the tests, the crutches, and ice packs were all free to me—essentially because I worked hard, I played hard, and most importantly—I served my country.

They're free to you too… if you qualify.

Unfortunately not all veterans are eligible for *free* health care through the VA. There is a whole list of people who are available for free healthcare, however, most on the list wouldn't be reading this book because they are far out from having separated from the military within the last fifteen years. However, the list does include vets who served in OEF, OIF, OND (which is the new OIF), former POW's, Purple Heart recipients, anyone with a 10% or higher disability rating, anyone who retired receiving a pension, and all of you Medal of Honor recipients.

If you don't fall into any of these categories you may not be eligible. If you don't fall into any of these categories, your available healthcare will be dependent on primarily your household income. You can find out more information on your eligibility dependent on household income here: http://nationalincomelimits.vaftl.us/.

Finally, if you happen to be a veteran with a service-connected disability rating from 10%-40% you will receive free medical care, *but* you will also have to pay for non-service connected medications. If you are rated at 50%-100%, you receive all care for free. Those who are at a 100% disability rating will also be eligible for free dental services through the VA.

The ins-and-outs of how the VA healthcare system works is intricate and complex when there are so many factors involved. It wasn't until I spoke with a credible source (a friend I served with who now works in the trenches of the VA), that I learned that I too had been wrong, for so many years, on my understanding of how the healthcare system worked. I learned this by recommending to a friend of mine (who needed radiation after having a brain tumor removed) to seek help from the VA since it was free, instead of paying his hospital bills out of pocket. He went through the process of calling around for more information and found out he made too much money in order to be helped, and that threw me into a whirlwind of confusion.

Everything I had thought was true about what *I* had known regarding how the VA healthcare system worked, *only* catered to *me*—because of *my* disability rating and priority grouping. My friend, a Marine whom I believe deserves some of the best care possible—and a person desperate to not break the bank on radiation in the civilian sector healthcare system, was *not* eligible because he had not been diligent in taking care of himself straight out of the Marine Corps. After getting both he and my friend who works in the VA in contact with each other, guidance was given in order to help ease the financial pain of what his sudden brain tumor would have continued to cause—to a household where there were three other mouths to feed.

Here is a separate instance of the VA helping someone very close to me. The best friend I went into boot camp with became a salty disgruntled veteran who wanted nothing to do with the Marine Corps once he got out. If I was around him and used any type of military jargon such as, "where's the head," or "it's 1600," I would receive something like "IT'S A FUCKING BATHROOM," and, "it's 4 FUCKING O'CLOCK... asshole." He didn't want to wear boots, go camping, shave, go on hikes... He wanted nothing to do with "it" if *it* reminded him of the Marine Corps. But one day he took his motorcycle to a closed track to race—and wrecked.

His leg broke in a way where his bone protruded through his skin and the suit he was wearing, and he had to be transported to a civilian hospital immediately. He was stuck in that hospital for a couple of weeks, and after all the surgeries—he found himself unable to walk and pretty badly damaged.

He also initially hadn't enrolled with the VA healthcare services, so his medical help wasn't as black and white as it should've been, but when he needed the help from the VA, they stepped in and wrote a letter to the hospital that had taken care of him, and helped with the brunt of the financial obligation. The VA continued to take care of him for the rest of his recovery, and to this day if he needs anything from them, they take full care of him.

His mindset had changed about his bond to the military because of how he'd been treated as a veteran. He had seen and had experienced firsthand the help we can receive as vets. His mindset changed about his perception of other fellow vets. A whole new respect for the system had been created, and it was because he allowed himself the opportunity to get better, to get healthy, and to take advantage of the incredible opportunity to live once again.

Over the years I've met individuals who have gone in with cancer that they were told would be terminal, and now they're well into remission. I've met individuals who've had their legs blown off, and now are running marathons. Whether you've got a chest cold, or Alzheimer's, let the VA take care of you. If not the VA, seek out any medical professional to get your body right. Give yourself an opportunity to be whole once again.

Remember: *Get fixed—or at least attempt to. We've still got a long road ahead of us.*

It's Ok to Swallow Your Pride

I'd been a Marine before war started, and well into a different era of a terror filled society. I have deployed as support, and volunteered many times to fight the fight with my family on the front lines, unfortunately (or fortunately) never having been taken serious enough to be FAP'd out (Fleet Assistance Program, where you get redistributed for a while to a different section, unit, or battalion). When I enlisted, I didn't know many Marines who had enlisted for the benefits. We enlisted to be bad-asses. We enlisted because we had a lot to prove. To whom? —Who knows... but I was surrounded by misfits, stubborn hard-headed assholes, bullies, jokesters and class clowns much like myself. We were misunderstood, but we were kind, caring and loyal. We were hard-working. We were society's lost boys, but to us, we had been found—we were the best of the best.

We all had a chip on our shoulder, and we all had something to prove.

While serving my country, I had found myself in my own troubles, and I have helped many out of theirs. While I was serving, I never really asked for help from others, but I never declined when others offered it. I was a man who could get shit done with nobody's help if I absolutely had to, and sometimes I was very eager to be something bigger than what I was. It wasn't always the right mindset for me to have, or the best thing for me to do—and I guess a lot of it was stubbornness.

I lived a life trying to prove that if I could do it, you could too. I live a lot like that today, but through these days—I've learned the value of asking for assistance.

My ex-wife had asked for a divorce not too long after I separated from the service, and I found myself essentially homeless, with very little money and no car. I had no job, no family to rely on, and the only thing I had going for me was that my buddy allowed me to stay on his couch while I was working things out. The news of the divorce and that she wanted me to leave her car at her parents house put my mind into problem solving mode.

How was I going to start over? How does anyone just start fresh?

During this shitty time of uncertainty, what I learned was that other people *are* willing to help you. People are out there that will give you the benefit of doubt, and help you get back on your feet.

Knowing that I needed a car, my buddy told me that his neighbor had an old beat up '81 Mercedes sitting in the alley not being used, and he thinks they're going to junk it. He kept telling me how much of a piece of shit it was, but at that point, I was not in a position to be choosey.

I asked the couple who owned it how much they wanted for it, and they told me the junkyard was offering them $300. I didn't have $300 dollars because I had been partying with my friends too much, thinking I was going back home to my wife who was still working on base in Japan. So I had to break down, swallow my pride, and ask around for assistance.

I first asked people whom I considered family—since they wouldn't judge me. Plus they were the ones partying with me, so I figured they wasted all the money I needed on rounds and rounds of beer, that the least they could do was get me into a car. They weren't able to help, so I asked a friend that I knew, but at the time wasn't close with enough to ask him for money—let alone a few hundred dollars. He gave me the $300 with no questions asked—simply on my word that I would get it back to him.

So I bought my first Mercedes for $300—and man it was a piece of shit. They had converted it into a Bio-Diesel, which was a fad for a while. People were changing their cars into used vegetable-oil-mobiles, and this had been one of them. Well the conversion ate through a few hoses, and the car had no radio, no A/C, and a huge hole in the driver side seat. Not to mention it took me approximately five whole seconds to make it from behind the crosswalk line to the other side of the intersection after the light turned green. But it did its job, and it allowed me to start my life over again.

With that car, I made it to every job interview I scheduled. It got me off the couch and into my first apartment. It helped move me from point A to point B for close to 7 months before literally falling apart on me. But by that time, I had secured my job, and had credibility for a used car loan… not to mention income to pay that loan.

That car was a blessing, and ultimately remains as a mascot in my life that stands for perseverance for when times are rough on me. I couldn't have done that without my friend's handout. And for that I am forever grateful and indebted to you Bryant.

The best part was that once I made my first $300 it immediately went to him, and when I handed it over, he said to me, "I never expected I'd see this back." So you see, assistance can come from anywhere. My friend and I didn't have that type of relationship before, and if we did I didn't know it. I had never asked to borrow any kind of money in that amount before, and to me it was a blessing. To him—it could've been another day, but what was another day to him meant the world to me. I mentioned it once before; A closed mouth never gets fed. Don't be afraid to swallow your pride, open your mouth, and ask for what you need.

Remember: *Help can come from the most unimaginable places. All you have to do is be willing to ask. Don't suffer and refuse to move forward in life because your pride is holding you back.*

How to Grow a Beard

LIFE AFTER A COURT-MARTIAL

Labor Day weekend 2007, I went out with my ex-wife and some friends of ours to a local area for Americans in Okinawa, Japan. That night changed my life.

At some point of the night, my friends and coworkers ended up fighting, and in an attempt to get them home safely, I was forced to help a friend out of a brutal beating he was receiving from at least five other people. The Japanese police came out and broke it up, sending my friend and I to jail to be questioned about the fight all night, and then thrown in a cell for the MPs to come get us.

The next morning we had been picked up from the Japanese police station and taken into the Air Force base's interrogation room. It was then I found out that I was being charged for crimes I didn't commit.

I had some issues before with under aged drinking, and a DUI extremely early in my career, but ever since those issues, my new life as a Non-Commissioned Officer was clean. And it wasn't one of those *clean-cause-you-didn't-get-caught* situations, I was clean cause I was trying to **_be_** the example.

You see, as long as I can remember during my time in the Marine Corps, I wanted to pin on Warrant Officer. Ever since I graduated boot camp, I had stored chevrons inside my cover of the next rank up, but once I picked up Sergeant—I started storing WO-1 insignia inside my cover, to remind me daily of my goals in the Corps.

I had a plan.

But this brutal fight that would leave me confused and ultimately—extremely depressed, interrupted that plan. You see, I was found guilty in a general court martial. The same GCM that I had twice turned down NJP for, and the same GCM that I *personally* requested in order for me to have a fair trial. As I said, I was earlier offered NJP twice, but I stuck by my guns and wanted to fight to maintain my clean record.

I had a plan.

Well, the storybook ending didn't happen. I sat in that courtroom confident that what was said in court was more than enough to have all charges dropped. That it was enough to finally have my life taken off pause, and finally have the opportunity to move forward from all this… but God had another plan. A jury of my "peers" found me guilty and I was looking into the face of 7 years in the brig.

God must have had bigger plans for me, because I was simply busted down two ranks, with a half month's pay taken from me for two months. I was allowed to keep my security clearance *and* I was allowed to serve the rest of my time out, pick up Corporal again, and leave the Corps with an Honorable Discharge. I essentially couldn't continue my career because I'd hit service time limitations. Even though that sucks, it was better than jail. Well, one would think. As I understand it, had I done just *one* day of jail time the courts would've been forced to review the case in full, but because I hadn't been sent to the brig, my case's review was not important enough to be reviewed in full, and so both my appeals did not go through.

So in regards to the court martial, I am still unsure of where I stand in the eyes of the law with it. Once I was charged, not one soul was able to tell me if this would be conceived as a felony or a misdemeanor. My military lawyer never got me an answer, and the civilian attorney, whom I hired for the appeal process, could not answer this question—because even though I was found guilty I didn't serve any jail time and I was still released with an Honorable Discharge, which is not awarded to felons.

Once I separated from the Corps in February 2010, I visited my Congresswoman, and was told it's not her job to handle military matters, and to my unfortunate luck, the military was done with the case as well. So I was forced to walk blindly as a civilian now—not knowing if my past would catch up to my present.

Initially it hadn't.

September 20th, 2010, I started my first job at a Civilian Contractor dealing with government equipment, taking me across the globe from base to base, working with international customers. The fact that I had a military clearance had helped me get my foot in the door, and not to mention, a few years after having worked at that company, I had been granted a renewal of my security clearance through the DoD to continue working at this company. I'd also been volunteering at the local Science Center with their dive program, which in order to volunteer, I had to be cleared by the Department of Justice.

So it seemed as if my past was not here to haunt me. Until one day 4 years later when I found out some pretty bad news.

I had finished my degree in Psychology and had now enrolled in the School Counseling Masters program at a local California State University. I was pursuing my long time dream of becoming a high school guidance counselor, and I was sincerely enjoying the journey. Along the way in my very first semester, I was offered a paid internship at a middle school, something very uncommon at this stage of the program, and I accepted. All I needed to do was provide some identification, tax documentation, and pass the background check.

The FBI check came back with my court martial on it, and LAUSD refused to make any exception. They wouldn't even take into account I had passed criteria for a government issued security clearance from the military, and a clearance to work with kids at the local Science center. To them, I was a risk, and they weren't willing to take a risk on me.

The snowball effect happened pretty fast. Not only was I not able to have the job, I wasn't allowed to volunteer at the school that offered me the job, and I was asked to leave the graduate program. My dreams of becoming a high school guidance counselor had vanished right in front of me in a matter of a week, and I learned that the only way I can get this situated, is for me to be granted a presidential pardon.

Imagine that the *one* clear road in your life had been abruptly taken from you, and you suddenly had no path in front of you to lead you home to safety. Like a blind man losing his walking stick, or a runner losing his legs... I'd lost my ability to move forward.

I'd lost my will *and* my drive. How long was I going to continue to be punished for something I should've never been charged for, especially when all I wanted to do in life was help young men and women become incredible young adults through guidance and giving them hope? I *knew* that my whole life's role was to be someone that will be there for their service, their cares, and their needs... for their safety and growth. How are you going to rob the kids from what I have to offer them?

I was down. I was depressed. I was a mess.

New Year's Eve 2014, two friends of mine came over to the house because my wife and I weren't going anywhere. We had just had our son that May, and he was too young… or we were too tired—but whatever the reason was, we decided to stay home. And so our doors were open to our friends and family.

Throughout the night I'd brought out the pity party of depression and guilt, and talked about the next step of how I'm going to try to rectify the situation by applying to the Marriage, Family, Therapy program, and my friend says to me, "why do you need to be a therapist or a counselor to help people?"

"Think about it," he says, "you're whole function as a person is to heal, to give back, to support and to be a leader. Your focus is wrong if you feel like you can *only* do that from a clinical or an office setting. You have to think outside the box of what it is you want to accomplish—and find a new way… a way that'll work for you. You could be a life coach."

He had broken the shackles that I placed on myself.

Initially I had some reserve about the term "life coach" but as I started researching and doing my homework on what it is I'd need to be fluent in, or what I'd need to study, I knew I could work this into my new life path. I knew that I would be able to affect more people in this model of "counseling" or support than I would in any school or clinic. I wouldn't be constrained to the institutions much stricter guidelines on how it is I would be able to help a student. I would be able to speak in pure truth, and with tough love, and not coddle the individuals that I knew would need more than simply someone with active listening skills.

I knew immediately that this was meant for me to stumble upon, and it changed my life.

Embracing the change of life I was going through, I was introduced to Hypnotherapy from a family friend, and it was then that the path became even more focused of how it is I can help the people I connect with most!

As I studied the mind through the principles of being able to connect the separation of the conscious and subconscious minds trough hypnosis, becoming a Certified Hypnotherapist gave me the tools and the freedoms to *really help* the vets coming home that are trying to adjust to life outside the service... really, it gave me the tools to help anyone that needed to focus on improving their lives.

We will all stumble and fall at some point. **Every single one of us**. And what I like to tell people is to not compare your problems to someone else's, because your problems are yours—and they're *huge*—because they affect you directly, personally, and emotionally. Other people's problems are huge too! And they affect them just as powerfully as your problems affect you, because those are their problems.

So when I thought that my court martial had won, and the military life I had lived had gotten the last laugh, I changed my life script. I turned the situation I was in, into a much better and much more free situation. I took the dark, and shined some light into it to find a gift. And this book is part of that gift. It's given me a way to continually help my brothers and sisters in arms. It's allowed me to continue to teach the lessons that I've learned, in hopes that I can help better someone's outcome, or make the path for many a little smoother.

During my road to get my Psychology degree, I fell in love with the concept of Maslow's Hierarchy of Needs. I often use it as a learning aid for where we are in life and how we set up the future for those who walk in our paths. It's a basic fundamental foundation of how we as people, as parents, and as guardians move up towards *self-actualization*, and create a stable foundation for those we love and care for.

Maslow's concept is that *physiological* needs need to be met first to create a solid base for growth through the next levels of *safety*, *love and belonging*, *esteem*, and finalizing at *self-actualization*. Basically he states that the basic functions and needs at different levels of life *must* be met before moving up through the higher levels of the pyramid. Basically, we cannot have self-esteem, confidence, or respect for others or ourselves unless we have love from someone other than ourselves. We can't have that love if we don't feel secure or have morals. We won't feel secure if we don't have food, water, or get sleep.

Once we establish these foundations, the people who follow in our footsteps are able to quickly move to the next level because we are giving them the gift of not having to learn everything for themselves. Because of our already learned life lessons, we are giving them the gift of not having to start from scratch at the bottom of the pyramid searching for food, water, and a place to sleep.

Maslow's concept requires us to work hard for what we have, learn from our lessons, and then teach others that to be where we are today was not easy. But because of our struggles, you—the individuals we care so much about who have not walked this path yet, can learn from our mistakes and move *forward and higher* up the pyramid *faster and more efficiently*—in order to pass on an even more solid and progressed base of a pyramid to the road to *actualization* for the ones who will walk the path after you.

If at any chance there are levels without sound foundations, then your pyramid will proverbially crumble. That's why as leaders of the future, we must learn from our lessons, and teach. Learn from our lessons, and give back to those walking the same path, or similar ones that we're finding ourselves on. That's why as a Marine Corps NCO, even though I look like a civilian now, I pass these lessons, tips, and tools down to you... to solidify those levels that have already been structured over and over again by many before you. And to shine light on the road for you to not have to learn these lessons the hard way and possibly give up on *your* hopes and dreams.

Too many military veterans separate from the service never to be heard from again. Too many people don't feel like there's anyone around to relate to. Too many people don't feel like there's life after their setbacks, just like I didn't think there was life after my court-martial, and I'm telling you right now—between you, me, God, and country—there *is* hope, there *is* support, and there *is* life after the military life you once knew... and I hope I can help you find it.

Remember: *Roadblocks will happen. Detours will pop up. Things are not always as smooth, easy, straightforward, or pleasant as we'd like them to be. But you are here right now, and you are a fighter. Stay cool, calm, and collected, and think outside the box. You are not alone, and it's okay to keep your mind and heart open for <u>help from others</u>. It's your time to do big things in life, and make a change—so do that. Do Big Things.*

The Yellow Brick Road Starts Here...

How to Grow a Beard

By now, you've realized that this book isn't about growing beards. I created that title to create symbolism for what it means for us... well, most of us to get out. Near the end of our enlistments, we dream for the day we can stop mandatorily shaving. We dream of the days that we're done with the 0400 formations, or even better the 0400 formation before the 0600 formation, before the 1000 piss test that runs into chow. We dream of the days we can store whatever liquor we want in our room, and have friends of the opposite sex legally in our rooms overnight without having to keep the door open. We dream of wearing different clothes everyday for work, and even the ability to say, "fuck this... I QUIT!"

Dreams are what keep us going through our everyday lives. In the service it's dreams of your future service self. Are you a top physical performer, or are you the next Chesty Puller? Are you just waiting out your 20 for retirement, then starting up a B&B in a resort town in Mexico, or are you dreaming of getting out and becoming a Doctor and joining Doctors without borders? Dreams are how we create our realities.

It's important to focus on the dreams that mean the most to you, because dreams *can* and *will* come true if you work toward them. Men and women leave the military every day. They receive their DD-214, and then they're let go into the wild to fend for themselves. Some may have no idea about the path they'd like to take, and might end up taking a small vacation from life in order to figure out what it is they'd like to move forward towards, and others have already secured a job and jumped right into the working world.

Some people can't take the civilian world right away, and find themselves re-enlisting, hopefully back into their previous MOS, but usually into a different job altogether. And some re-enlist to a completely different service.

The civilian world is a different place, and the symbolism of growing a beard is created to represent the separation of you and the service you've given your life to. The creation of a new identity, and the obtainment of your dreams, no matter how big or small. The beard represents an achievement that you have gone through one of the most in-depth classes on maturing, and how to be a functional adult, and that you've graduated in order to make the world a different place.

Your beard may be trimmed and manicured, or it may be big and bushy. You may only like the 5 o'clock shadow, or you may choose to remain fresh faced, with a fresh haircut on Monday morning, as you've been accustomed to for so many years before today. Whatever you choose to do out in the civilian world—find yourself. Be—yourself. Find a purpose. Find *your* purpose.

Don't settle for less than what you feel you're worth. That's is true with work, homes, lovers, education... anything. You've deserved this for a long time, and now that it's a reality, what are you going to do with it?

Just remember that as a civilian, you are not protected by your squadrons, your NCOIC, or your battle buddy any longer. As hardened and big and bad-ass as we think we are, when we step out of those E-1 to O-9 ranks and into the Mr. and Ms/Mrs. Ranks, we become fragile and vulnerable.

Every single person who serves experiences civilian life a little differently than others, however I guarantee one thing; whether you hate being in the service and are counting down your days, or you have your head in a pillow crying about how you don't want to get out... both those types of people at some point will agree that life on the outside is different, and both may even proclaim how much you hate civilian mentality.

So find yourself. If you need help—get it. If you need fixing... fix it. You may feel like you're alone sometimes, but there are others around who understand what it is you need and what it is you're looking for. I implore you to find a single person, or a group of people to help this transition be smooth for you. I plead with you to keep in touch with the people who wanted you to succeed while you were in. I encourage you to never forget who you are—a warrior, a peace-keeper, a brother, a sister... never forget that you are you.

With that, I wish you well on your journey to find out who the civilian version of yourself is. I know that if you keep the lessons learned in this book in mind, you can overcome any obstacle you'll find yourself in during your search for "normality." You've made it this far, and you've got an upper hand on those around you who didn't serve. Remember to do big things in life, and success usually doesn't happen overnight. Remember that <u>Redwoods were seeds once too</u>.

Remember: *Transition <u>is</u> hard—mentally and physically. You're not invincible out here. New game. New rules. But know that you're not the first to do it, so know that you don't have to do it alone. Allow yourself to go through the motions of getting to learn who it is that you are, and do something great in life. It's your story—how will it play out?*

Appendix

APPENDIX*

GENERAL

Veterans Association
http://www.va.gov/
1(800) 827-1000

Veteran Benefits
http://www.benefits.va.gov/benefits/

Military 1 Source: "One Stop Shop" for most questions (HIGHLY RECCOMENDED)
http://www.militaryonesource.mil/
1 (800) 342-9647

VA Home Loan information
http://www.benefits.va.gov/homeloans

Transitional Assistance Program
https://www.dodtap.mil/

HEALTH

VA Health Benefits
http://www.va.gov/healthbenefits/apply/returning_servicemembers.asp

My Health Vet (a must register site**)**
https://www.myhealth.va.gov

Annual Income Thresholds (Used to determine the amount of healthcare you can receive through the VA, if you don't qualify for free healthcare)
http://nationalincomelimits.vaftl.us/

Tricare
http://tricare.mil/

VA Compensation
http://www.benefits.va.gov/compensation/index.asp

APPENDIX

Education

Free Application for Federal Student Aid
https://fafsa.ed.gov/

Joint Service Transcript (formally know as the SMART)
https://jst.doded.mil/smart/welcome.do

VA Education Benefit Information
http://www.benefits.va.gov/gibill/

Help Hotlines

Veterans Crisis Line
https://www.veteranscrisisline.net/
1 (800) 273- 8255, press 1

DoD Sexual Assault Helpline
https://www.safehelpline.org/
1 (877) 995-5247

Military Crisis Line (for service members and their families)
https://www.veteranscrisisline.net/ActiveDuty.aspx
1 (800) 273-8255

National Domestic Violence Hotline
http://www.thehotline.org/
1 (800) 799-7233

Child National Abuse Hotline
https://www.childhelp.org/hotline/
1 (800) 422-4453

*Websites and telephone numbers are subject to change over time.

*Remember to do your own research for your personal situation. Use these resources as reference only.

How to Grow a Beard

ABOUT THE AUTHOR

Robert Graves is a Life Coach and Certified Hypnotherapist, living in Southern California, focusing on Athletic Peak Performance training, and Military Transition Assistance.

He is a husband, a father, a veteran, and a friend to all. He has dedicated his civilian time to learning and pursuing ways to help those in need, with special attention to adolescents, veterans, and those suffering from Auto-Immune Diseases such as Cancer and Multiple Sclerosis.

Leaving behind his 10-year Marine Corps career, he vowed to continue to help his brothers and sisters-in-arms, in order for those who served to become successful on the outside of the military.

Connect with me:
Website: www.CoachGraves.com
Twitter: @How2GrowABeard
Facebook: www.facebook.com/HowToGrowABeardBook/
Periscope: @CoachGraves
Blab: @LIVECoachGraves

Made in the USA
San Bernardino, CA
28 April 2016